Ex Líbris

50P

WORKING FOR GOD

A sequel to
WAITING ON GOD

Andrew Murray

MARSHALL, MORGAN & SCOTT

Lakeland
Marshall, Morgan & Scott
a member of the Pentos group
1 Bath Street, London EC1V 9LB

This edition copyright Marshall, Morgan & Scott 1979

ISBN 0 551 00810 5

Printed in Great Britain by
Hunt Barnard Printing Ltd., Aylesbury, Bucks

Contents

Introduction

The object of this little book is first of all to remind all Christian workers of the greatness and the glory of the work in which God gives a share. It is nothing less than that work of bringing men back to their God, at which God finds His highest glory and blessedness. As we see that it is God's own work we have to work out, that He works it through us, that in our doing it His glory rests on us and we glorify Him, we shall count it our joy to give ourselves to live only and wholly for it.

The aim of the book at the same time is to help those who complain, and perhaps do not even know to complain, that they are apparently labouring in vain, to find out what may be the cause of so much failure. God's work must be done in God's way, and in God's power. It is spiritual work, to be done by spiritual men, in the power of the Spirit. The clearer our insight into, and the more complete our submission to, God's laws of work, the surer and the richer will be our joy and our reward in it.

Along with this I have had in view the great number of Christians who practically take no real part in the service of their Lord. They have never understood that as the chief characteristic of the Divine life in God and Christ is love and its work of blessing men, the Divine life in us can show itself in no other way. I have tried to show that it is God's will that every believer without exception, whatever be his position in life, gives himself wholly to live and work for God.

I have also written in the hope that some, who have the training of others in Christian life and work, may find thoughts that will be of use to them in teaching the imperative duty, the urgent need, the Divine blessedness of a life given to God's service, and to waken within the consciousness of the power that works in them, even the Spirit and power of Christ Himself.

To the great host of workers in the Church, I lovingly offer these meditations, with the fervent prayer that God, the Great Worker, may make us true Fellow-workers with Himself.

ANDREW MURRAY

Waiting and Working

'They that wait upon the Lord shall *renew their strength*. Neither hath the eye seen, O God, beside Thee, which worketh for him that *waiteth for Him*.' – Isa. 40:31, 64:4.

Here we have two texts in which the connection between waiting and working is made clear. In the first we see that waiting brings the needed strength for working – that it fits for joyful and unwearied work. 'They that wait on the Lord shall renew their strength; they shall mount up on eagles' wings; they shall run, and not be weary; they shall walk, and not faint.' Waiting on God has its value in this: it makes us strong in work for God. The second reveals the secret of this strength. 'God worketh for him that waiteth for Him.' The waiting on God secures the working of God for us and in us, out of which our work must spring. The two passages teach the great lesson, that as waiting on God lies at the root of all true working for God, so working for God must be the fruit of all true waiting on Him. Our great need is to hold the two sides of the truth in perfect conjunction and harmony.

There are some who say they wait upon God, but who do not work for Him. For this there may be various reasons. One confuses true waiting on God (living in direct intercourse with Him as the Living One), and the devotion to Him of the energy of the whole being, with the slothful, helpless waiting that excuses itself from all work until God, by some special impulse, has made work easy. Another waits on God more truly, regarding it as one of the highest exercises of the Christian life, and yet has never understood that at the root of all true waiting there must lie the surrender and the readiness to be wholly fitted for God's use in the service of men. Still another is ready to work as well as wait, but is looking for some great inflow of the Spirit's power to enable him to do mighty works, while he forgets that as a believer he already has the Spirit of Christ dwelling in him; that more grace is only given to those who are faithful in the little; and that it is only in working that we can be taught by the Spirit how to do the greater works. All such, and all Christians, need to learn that waiting has working for its object, that it is only in working that waiting can attain its full perfection and blessedness. It is as we elevate working for God to its true place, as the highest exercise of spiritual privilege and power, that the absolute need and the divine blessing of waiting on God can be fully known.

On the other hand, there are some, there are many, who work for God but know little of what it is to wait on Him. They have been led to take up Christian work, under the impulse of natural or religious feeling, at the bidding of a pastor or a society, with but very little sense of what a holy thing it is to work for God. They do not know that *God's work can only be done in God's strength, by God Himself working in us*. They have never learnt that, just as the Son of God could do nothing of Himself, but that the Father in Him did the work, as He lived in continual dependence before Him, so, and much more, the believer can do nothing but as God works in him. They do not understand that it is only as in utter weakness we depend upon Him that His power can rest on us. And so they have no conception of a continual waiting on God as being one of the first and essential conditions of successful work. And Christ's Church and the world are sufferers today, not only because so many of its members are not working for God, but because so much working for God is done without waiting on God.

Among the members of the body of Christ there is a great diversity of gifts and operations. Some, who are confined to their homes by reason of sickness or other duties, may have more time for waiting on God than opportunity of direct working for Him. Others, who are overpressed by work, find it very difficult to find time and quiet for waiting on Him. These may mutually supply each other's lack. Let those who have time for waiting on God definitely link themselves to some who are working. Let those who are working as definitely claim the aid of those to whom the special ministry of waiting on God has been entrusted. So will the unity and the health of the body be maintained. So will those who wait know that the outcome will be power for work, and those who work, that their only strength is the grace obtained by waiting. So will God work for His Church that waits on Him.

Let us pray that as we proceed in these meditations on working for God, the Holy Spirit may show us how sacred and how urgent our calling is to work, how absolute our dependence is upon God's strength to work in us, how sure it is that those who wait on Him shall renew their strength, and how we shall find waiting on God and working for God to be indeed inseparably one.

1. It is only as God works for me, and in me, that I can work for Him.

2. All His work for me is through His life in me.

3. He will most surely work, if I wait on Him.

4. All His working for me, and my waiting on Him, has but one aim, to fit me for His work of saving men.

Good Works
the Light of the World

'Ye are the light of the world. Let your light shine before men, that they may see your *good works*, and glorify your Father which is in heaven.' – MATT. 5:14, 16.

A light is always meant for the use of those who are in darkness, that by it they may see. The sun lights up the darkness of this world. A lamp is hung in a room to give it light. The Church of Christ is the light of men. The God of this world has blinded their eyes; Christ's disciples are to shine into their darkness and give them light. As the rays of light stream forth from the sun and scatter that light all about, so the good works of believers are the light that streams out from them to conquer the surrounding darkness, with its ignorance of God and estrangement from Him.

What a high and holy place is thus given to our good works. What power is attributed to them. How much depends upon them. They are not only the light and health and joy of our own life, but in every deed the means of bringing lost souls out of darkness into God's marvellous light. They are even more. They not only bless men, but they glorify God, in leading men to know Him as the author of the grace seen in His children. We propose studying the teaching of Scripture in regard to good works, and specially all work done directly for God

13

and His kingdom. Let us listen to what these words of the Master have to teach us.

The aim of good works. It is, that God may be glorified. You remember how our Lord said to the Father: 'I have glorified Thee on the earth, I have finished the work which Thou gavest Me to do.' We read more than once of His miracles, that the people glorified God. It was because what He had wrought was manifestly by a Divine power. It is when our good works are something more than the ordinary virtues of refined men, and bear the impress of God upon them, that men will glorify God. They must be the good works of which the Sermon on the Mount is the embodiment – a life of God's children, doing more than others, seeking to be perfect as their Father in heaven is perfect. This glorifying of God by men may not mean conversion, but it is a preparation for it when an impression favourable to God has been made. The works prepare the way for the words, and are an evidence of the reality of the Divine truth that is taught, while without them the word is powerless.

The whole world was made for the glory of God. Christ came to redeem us from sin and bring us back to serve and glorify Him. Believers are placed in the world with this one object, that they may let their light shine in good works, so as to win men to God. As truly as the light of the sun is meant to lighten the world, the good works of God's children are meant to be the light of those who know and love not God. What need that we form a right conception of what good works are, as bearing the mark of something heavenly and divine, and having a power to compel the admission that God is in them.

The power of good works. Of Christ it is written: 'In Him was life, and the life was the light of men.' The Divine life gave out a Divine light. Of His disciples Christ

14

said: 'If any man follow Me, he shall not walk in darkness, but have the *light of life*.' Christ is our life and light. When it is said to us, 'Let your light shine', the deepest meaning is, let Christ, who dwells in you, shine. As in the power of His life you do your good works, your light shines out to all who see you. And because Christ in you is your light, your works, however humble and feeble they be, can carry with them a power of Divine conviction. The measure of the Divine power which works them in you will be the measure of the power working in those who see them. Give way, O child of God, to the Life and Light of Christ dwelling in you, and men will see in your good works that for which they will glorify your Father which is in heaven.

The urgent need of good works in believers. As needful as that the sun shines every day, yea, more so, is it that every believer lets his light shine before men. For this we have been created anew in Christ, to hold forth the Word of Life as lights in the world. Christ needs you urgently, my brother, to let His light shine through you. Perishing men around you need your light, if they are to find their way to God. God needs you, to let His glory be seen through you.

Let us undertake the study of what working for God is, and what good works are as part of this, with the desire to follow Christ fully, and so to have the light of life shining into our hearts and lives, and from us on all around.

1. '*Ye are the light of the world!*' The words express the calling of the Church as a whole. The fulfilment of her duty will depend upon the faithfulness with which each individual member loves and lives for those around him.

2. In all our efforts to waken the Church to evangelise

15

the world, our first aim must be to raise the standard of life for the individual believer of the teaching: As truly as a candle only exists with the object of giving light in the darkness, *the one object of your existence is to be a light to men.*

3. Pray God by His Holy Spirit to reveal it to you that you have nothing to live for but to let the light and love of the life of God shine upon souls.

Son, Go Work

'Son, *go work* today in my vineyard.' – MATT. 21:28.

The father had two sons. To each he gave the command to go and work in his vineyard. The one went, the other went not. God has given the command and the power to every child of His to work in His vineyard, with the world as the field. The majority of God's children are not working for Him, and the world is perishing.

Of all the mysteries that surround us in the world, is not one of the strangest and most incomprehensible this – that after 1800 years the very name of the Son of God should be unknown to the larger half of the human race.

Just consider what this means. To restore the ruin sin had wrought, God, the Almighty Creator, actually sent His own Son to the world to tell men of His love, and to bring them His life and salvation. When Christ made His disciples partakers of that salvation, and the unspeakable joy it brings, it was with the express understanding that they should make it known to others, and so be the lights of the world. He spoke of all who through them should believe, having the same calling. He left the world with the distinct instruction to carry the Gospel to every creature, and teach all nations to observe all that He had commanded. He at the same time gave the definite assurance that all power for this work was in

2

Him, that He would always be with His people, and that by the power of His Holy Spirit they would be able to witness to Him to the ends of the earth. And what do we see now? After 1800 years two-thirds of the human race have scarce heard the name of Jesus. And of the other third, the larger half is still as ignorant as if they had never heard.

Consider again what this means. All these dying millions, whether in Christendom or heathendom, have an interest in Christ and His salvation. They have a right to Him. Their salvation depends on their knowing Him. He could change their lives from sin and wretchedness to holy obedience and heavenly joy. Christ has a right to them. It would make His heart glad to have them come and be blessed in Him. But they and He are dependent on the service of His people to be the connecting link to bring them and Him together. And yet what His people do is as nothing to what needs to be done, to what could be done, to what ought to be done.

Just consider yet once again what this means. What a revelation of the state of the Church. The great majority of those who are counted believers are doing nothing towards making Christ known to their fellow-men. Of the remainder, the majority are doing so little, and that little so ineffectually, by reason of the lack of whole-hearted devotion, that they can hardly be said to be giving themselves to their Lord's service. And of the remaining portion, who have given themselves and all they have to Christ's service, so many are occupied with the hospital work of teaching the sick and the weakly in the Church, that the strength left free for aggressive work, and going forth to conquer the world, is terribly reduced. And so, with a finished salvation, and a loving Redeemer, and a Church set apart to carry life and blessing to men, the millions are still perishing.

There can be no question to the Church of more intense and pressing importance than this: What can be done to waken believers to a sense of their holy calling, and to make them see that *to work for God*, that to offer themselves as instruments *through whom God can do His work*, ought to be the one aim of their life? The vain complaints that are continually heard of a lack of enthusiasm for God's kingdom on the part of the great majority of Christians, the vain attempts to waken anything like an interest in missions proportionate to their claim, or Christ's claim, make us feel that nothing less is needed than a revival that shall be a revolution, and shall raise even the average Christian to an entirely new type of devotion. No true change can come until the truth is preached and accepted, that the law of the kingdom is: *Every believer to live only and wholly for God's service and work.*

The father who called his sons to go and work in his vineyard did not leave it to their choice to do as much or as little as they chose. They lived in his home; they were his children, he counted on what they would give him, their time and strength. This God expects of His children. Until it is understood that each child of God is to give His whole heart to his Father's interest and work, until it is understood that every child of God is to be a worker for God, the evangelisation of the world cannot be accomplished. Let every reader listen, and the Father will say to him personally: 'Son, go work in My vineyard.'

1. Why is it that stirring appeals on behalf of missions often have so little permanent result? Because the command with its motives is brought to men who have not learned that absolute devotion and immediate obedience to their Lord is of the essence of true salvation.

2. If it is once seen, and confessed, that the lack of interest in missions is the token of a low and sickly Christian life, all who plead for missions will make it their first aim to proclaim the calling of every believer to live wholly for God. Every missionary meeting will be a consecration meeting to seek and surrender to the Holy Spirit's power.

3. The average standard of holiness and devotion cannot be higher abroad than at home, or in the Church at large than in individual believers.

4. Every one cannot go abroad, or give his whole time to direct work; but everyone, whatever his calling or circumstances, can give his whole heart to live for souls and the spread of the kingdom.

To Each one his Work

'As a man sojourning in another country, having given authority to his servants, *to each one his work*, commanded the porter also to watch.' – MARK 13:34.

What I have said in a previous chapter of the failure of the Church to do her Master's work, or even clearly to insist upon the duty of its being done by every member, has often led me to ask the question, What must be done to arouse the Church to a right sense of her calling? This little book is an attempt to give the answer. Working for God must take a very different and much more definite place in our teaching and training of Christ's disciples than it has done.

In studying the question I have been very much helped by the life and writings of a great educationalist. The opening sentence of the Preface to his biography tells us: 'Edward Thring was unquestionably the most original and striking figure in the schoolmaster world of his time in England.' He himself attributes his own power and success to the prominence he gave to a few simple principles, and the faithfulness with which he carried them out at any sacrifice. I have found them as suggestive in regard to the work of preaching as of teaching, and to state them will help to make plain some of the chief lessons this book is meant to teach.

The root-principle that distinguished his teaching from what was current at the time was this: *Every boy in school, the dullest, must have the same attention as the cleverest.* At Eton, where he had been educated, and had come out first, he had seen the evil of the opposite system. The school kept up its name by training a number of men for the highest prizes, while the majority were neglected. He maintained that this was dishonest: there could be no Truth in a school which did not care for all alike. Every boy had some gift; every boy needed special attention; every boy could, with care and patience, be fitted to know and fulfil his mission in life.

Apply this to the Church. Every believer, the feeblest as much as the strongest, has the calling to live and work for the kingdom of his Lord. Every believer has equally a claim on the grace and power of the Holy Spirit, according to his gifts, to fit him for this work. And every believer has a right to be taught and helped by the Church for the service our Lord expects of him. It is when this truth, *every believer, the feeblest, to be trained as a worker for God*, gets its true place, that there can be any thought of the Church fulfilling its mission. Not one can be missed, because the Master gave to every one his work.

Another of Thring's principles was this: *It is a law of nature that work is pleasure.* See to make it voluntary and not compulsory. Do not lead the boys blindfold. Show them why they have to work, what its value will be, what interest can be awakened in it, what pleasure may be found in it. A little time, stolen, as he says, for that purpose, from the ordinary teaching, will be more than compensated for by the spirit which will be thrown into the work.

What a field is opened out here for the preacher of the gospel in the charge he has of Christ's disciples. To un-

22

fold before them the greatness, the glory, the Divine blessedness of the work to be done. To show its value, in the carrying out of God's will, and gaining His approval in our becoming the benefactors and saviours of the perishing; in developing that spiritual vigour, that nobility of character, that spirit of self-sacrifice which leads to the true bearing of Christ's image.

A third truth Thring insisted on specially was *the need of inspiring the belief in the possibility, yea, the assurance of success in gaining the object of pursuit*. That object is not much knowledge; not every boy can attain to this. The drawing out and cultivation of the power there is in himself and this alone is true education. As a learner's powers of observation grow under true guidance and teaching, and he finds within himself a source of power and pleasure he never knew before, he feels a new self beginning to live, and the world around him gets a new meaning. 'He becomes conscious of an infinity of un-suspected glory in the midst of which we go about our daily tasks, becomes lord of an endless kingdom full of light and pleasure and power.'

If this be the law and blessing of a true education, what light is shed on the calling of all teachers and leaders in Christ's Church! The *know ye nots* of Scripture – that ye are the temple of God – that Christ is in you – that the Holy Spirit dwelleth in you – acquire a new meaning. It tells us that the one thing that needs to be wakened in the hearts of Christians is the faith 'in the power that work-eth in us'. As one comes to see the worth and the glory of the work to be done, as one believes in the possibility of being able to do that work well; as one learns to trust a Divine energy, the very power and spirit of God working in one; 'he will, in the fullest sense, become conscious of a new life, with an infinity of unsuspected glory in the midst of which we go about our daily task, and become

23

lord of an endless kingdom full of light and pleasure and power.'

This is the royal life to which God has called all His people. The true Christian is one who knows God's power working in himself, and finds it his true joy to have the very life of God flow into him, and through him, and out from him to those around.

1. We must learn to believe in the power of littles – of the value of every individual believer. As men are saved one by one, they must be trained one by one for work.

2. We must believe that work for Christ can become as natural, as much an attraction and a pleasure in the spiritual as in the natural world.

3. We must believe and teach that every believer can become an effective worker in his sphere. Are you seeking to be filled with love to souls?

To Each
according to his Ability

'The kingdom of heaven is as when a man, going into another country, called his own servants, and delivered them his goods. And unto one he gave five talents, to another two, to another one; *to each according to his several ability*.' – MATT. 25:14.

In the parable of the talents we have a most instructive summary of our Lord's teaching in regard to the work He has given to His servants to do. He tells us of His going to heaven and leaving His work on earth to the care of His Church; of His giving every one something to do, however different the gifts might be; of His expecting to get back His money with interest; of the failure of him who had received least; and of what it was that led to that terrible neglect.

'*He called his own servants and delivered unto them his goods, and went on his journey*.' This is literally what our Lord did. He went to heaven, leaving His work with all His goods to the care of His Church. His goods were the riches of His grace, the spiritual blessings in heavenly places, His word and Spirit, with all the power of His life on the throne of God – all these He gave in trust to His servants, to be used by them in carrying on His work on

25

earth. The work he had begun they were to prosecute. As some rich merchant leaves Cape Town to reside in London, while his business is carried on by trustworthy servants, our Lord took His people into partnership with Himself, and entrusted His work on earth entirely to their care. Through their neglect it would suffer; their diligence would be His enrichment. Here we have the true root-principle of Christian service; Christ has made Himself dependent for the extension of His kingdom on the faithfulness of His people.

'*Unto one he gave five talents, to another two, to another one; to each according to his several ability.*' Though there was a difference in the measure, every one received a portion of the master's goods. It is in connection with the service we are to render to each other that we read of 'the grace given to each of us according to the measure of the gift of Christ'. This truth, that every believer without exception has been set apart to take an active part in the work of winning the world for Christ, has almost been lost sight of. Christ was first a son, then a servant. Every believer is first a child of God, then a servant. It is the highest honour of a son to be a servant, to have the father's work entrusted to him. Neither the home nor the foreign missionary work of the Church will ever be done aright until every believer feels that the one object of his being in the world is to work for the kingdom. The first duty of the servants in the parable was to spend their life in caring for their master's interests.

'*After a long time the lord of those servants cometh and maketh a reckoning with them.*' Christ keeps watch over the work He has left to be done on earth; His kingdom and glory depend upon it. He will not only hold reckoning when He comes again to judge, but comes unceasingly to inquire of His servants as to their welfare and work. He comes to approve and encourage, to correct and warn. By His word and Spirit He asks us to say whether we are using our talents diligently, and, as His devoted servants, living only and entirely for His work. Some He finds labouring diligently, and to them He frequently says: 'Enter into the joy of thy Lord.' Others He sees discouraged, and them He inspires with new hope. Some He finds working in their own strength; these He reproves. Still others He finds sleeping or hiding their talent; to such His voice speaks in solemn warning: 'from him that hath shall be taken away even that he hath.' Christ's heart is in His work; every day He watches over it with the intensest interest; let us not disappoint Him nor deceive ourselves.

'*Lord, I was afraid and hid thy talent in the earth.*' That the man of the one talent should have been the one to fail, and to be so severely punished, is a lesson of deep solemnity. It calls the Church to beware lest, by neglecting to teach the feebler ones, the one-talent men, that their service too is needed, she allow them to let their gifts lie unused. In teaching the great truth that every branch is to bear fruit, special stress must be laid on the danger of thinking that this can only be expected of the strong and advanced Christian. When Truth reigns in a school, the most backward pupil has the same attention as the more clever. Care must be taken that the feeblest Christians receive special training, so that they too may joyfully have their share in the service of their Lord and all the blessedness it brings. If Christ's work is to be done, not one can be missed.

'*Lord, I knew that thou art a hard man, and I was afraid.*' Wrong thoughts of God, looking upon His service as that of a hard master, are one chief cause of failure in service. If the Church is indeed to care for the feeble ones, for the one-talent servants, who are apt to be discouraged by reason of their conscious weakness, we must teach them what God says of the sufficiency of grace and the certainty of success.

1. The power of the Holy Spirit within a Christian fits him for the work to which God has called him.

2. Work is joy and health and strength.

3. Unbelief lies at the root of sloth. Faith opens the eyes to see the blessedness of service, its rich reward, and the sufficiency of God's grace.

Life and Work

'My meat is to do the will of Him that sent Me, and to accomplish *His work*. I must *work the works of Him* that sent Me. I have glorified Thee on the earth; I have *finished the work* Thou gavest Me to do. And now, O Father, glorify Me with Thyself.' – JOHN 5:34, 9:4, 17:4.

'Work is the highest form of existence.' The highest manifestation of the Divine Being is in His work. Read carefully again the words of our Blessed Lord at the head of the chapter, and see what Divine glory there is in work. In His work Christ showed forth His own glory and that of the Father. It was because of the work He had done, and because in it He had glorified the Father, that He claimed to share the glory of the Father in heaven. The greater works He was *to do* in answer to the prayer of the disciples was, that the Father might be glorified in the Son. Work is indeed the highest form of existence, the highest manifestation of the Divine glory in the Father and in His Son.

What is true of God is true of His creature. Life is movement, is action, and reveals itself in what it accomplishes. The bodily life, the intellectual, the moral, the spiritual life – individual, social, national life – each of these is judged of by its work. The character and quality of the work depends on the life: as the life, so the work. And, on the other hand, the life depends on the work; without this there can be no full development and manifestation and perfecting of the life: as the work, so the life.

This is specially true of the spiritual life – the life of the Spirit in us. There may be a great deal of religious work with its external activities, the outcome of human will and effort, with but little true worth and power, because the Divine life is feeble. When the believer does not know that Christ is living in him, does not know the Spirit and power of God working in him, there may be much earnestness and diligence, with little that lasts for eternity. There may, on the contrary, be much external weakness and apparent failure, and yet results that prove that the life is indeed of God.

The work depends upon the life. And the life depends on the work for its growth and perfection. All life has a destiny; it cannot accomplish its purpose without work; life is perfected by work. The highest manifestation of its hidden nature and power comes out in its work. And so work is the great factor by which the hidden beauty and the Divine possibilities of the Christian life are brought out.

Work must be restored to its right place in God's scheme of the Christian life as in very deed the highest form of existence. To be the intelligent willing channel of the power of God, to be capable of working the very work of God, to be animated by the Divine Spirit of love, and in that to be allowed to work life and blessing to men; it is this that gives nobility to life, because it is for this that we were created in the image of God. As God never for a moment ceases to work His work of love and blessing in us and through us, so our working out what He works in us is our highest proof of being created anew in His likeness.

If God's purpose with the perfection of the individual believer, with the appointment of His Church as the body of Christ to carry on His work of winning back a rebellious world to His allegiance and love, is to be carried out, working for God must have much greater prominence given to it as the true glory of our Christian calling. Every believer must be taught that, as work is the only perfect manifestation, and therefore the perfection of life in God and throughout the world, so our work is to be our highest glory. Shall it be so in our lives?

If this is to come, we must remember two things. The one is that it can only come by beginning to work. Those who have not had their attention specially directed to it cannot realise how great the temptation is to make work a matter of thought and prayer and purpose, without its really being *done*. It is easier to hear than to think, easier to think than to speak, easier to speak than to act. We may listen and accept and admire God's will, and in our prayer profess our willingness to do – and yet not actually *do*. Let us, with such measure of grace as we have, and much prayer for more, take up our calling as God's working men, and do good hard work for Him. Doing is the best teacher. If you want to know how to do a thing, begin and do it.

Then you will feel the need of the second thing I wish to mention, and be made capable of understanding it – that there is sufficient grace in Christ for all the work you have to do. You will see with ever-increasing gladness how He the Head works all in you the member, and how work for God may become your closest and fullest fellowship with Christ, your highest participation in the power of His risen and glorified life.

1. Life and work: beware of separating them. The more work you have, the more your work appears a failure. The more unfit you feel for work, take all the more time and care to have your inner life renewed in close fellowship with God.

2. Christ liveth in me – is the secret of joy and hope, and also of power for work. Care for the life, the life will care for the work. 'Be filled with the Spirit.'

The Father abiding in Me doeth the Work

'Jesus answered them, *My Father worketh* even until now, *and I work.*' – JOHN 5:17–20.
'Believest thou not that I am in the Father, and the Father in Me? the words that I speak I speak not of Myself: but the Father abiding in Me *doeth* the work.' – JOHN 14:10.

Jesus Christ became man that He might show us what a true man is, how God meant to live and work in man, and how man may find his life and do his work in God. In words like those above, our Lord opens up the inner mystery of His life, and discloses to us the nature and the deepest secret of His working. He did not come to the world to work instead of the Father; the Father was ever working – 'worketh even until now'. Christ's work was the fruit, the earthly reflection of the Heavenly Father working. And it was not as if Christ merely saw and copied what the Father willed or did: 'the Father *abiding in Me* doeth the work.' Christ did all His work in the power of the Father dwelling and working in Him. So complete and real was His dependence on the Father, that, in expounding it to the Jews, He used the strong expressions (5:19, 30): 'The Son can do nothing of Himself, but what He seeth the Father doing'; 'I can do

3

nothing of Myself.' As literally as what He said is true of us, 'Apart from Me ye can do nothing,' is it true of Him too. 'The Father abiding in Me doeth the work.'

Jesus Christ became man that He might show us what true man is, what the true relation between man and God, what the true way of serving God and doing His work. When we are made new creatures in Christ Jesus, the life we receive is the very life that was and is in Christ, and it is only by studying His life on earth that we know how we are to live. His dependence on the Father is the law of our dependence on Him and on the Father through Him.

Christ counted it no humiliation to be able to do nothing of Himself, to be always and absolutely dependent on the Father. He counted it His highest glory, because so all His works were the works of the all-glorious God in Him. When shall we understand that to wait on God, to bow before Him in perfect helplessness, and let Him work all in us, is our true nobility, and the secret of the highest activity? This alone is the true Son-life, the true life of every child of God. As this life is known and maintained, the power for work will grow, because the soul is in the attitude in which God can work in us, as the God who 'worketh for him that waiteth on Him'. It is the ignorance or neglect of the great truths that there can be no true work for God *but as God works it in us*, and that God cannot work in us fully *but as we live in absolute dependence on Him*, that is the explanation of the universal complaint of so much Christian activity with so little real result. The revival which many are longing and praying for must begin with this: the return of Christian ministers and workers to their true place before God – in Christ and like Christ, one of complete dependence and continual waiting on God to work in them.

Let me invite all workers, young and old, successful or

disappointed, full of hope or full of fear, to come and learn from our Lord Jesus the secret of true work for God. 'My Father worketh, and I work'; 'The Father abiding in Me doeth the works.' Divine Fatherhood means that God is all, and gives all, and works all. Divine Sonship means continual dependence on the Father, and the reception, moment by moment, of all the strength needed for His work. Try to grasp the great truth that because 'it is God who worketh all in all', your one need is, in deep humility and weakness, to wait for and to trust in His working. Learn from this that God can only work in us as He dwells in us. 'The Father abiding in Me doeth the works.' Cultivate the holy sense of God's continual nearness and presence, of your being His temple, and of His dwelling in you. Offer yourself for Him to work in you all His good pleasure. You will find that work, instead of being a hindrance, can become your greatest incentive to a life of fellowship and childlike dependence.

At first it may appear as if the waiting for God to work will keep you back from your work. It may indeed – but only to bring the greater blessing, when you have learned the lesson of faith, that counts on His working even when you do not feel it. You may have to do your work in weakness and fear and much trembling. You will know that it is all, that the excellency of the power may be of God and not of us. As you know yourself better and God better, you will be content that it should ever be – His strength made perfect in our weakness.

1. 'The Father abiding in Me doeth the work.' There is the same law for the Head and the member, for Christ and the believer. 'It is the same God that worketh all in all.'

2. The Father not only worked in the Son when He was

on earth, but now, too, that He is in heaven. It is as we *believe in Christ in the Father's working in Him*, that we shall do the greater works. See John 14:10–12.

3. It is as the indwelling God, the Father abiding in us, that God works in us. Let the life of God in the soul be clear, the work will be sure.

4. Pray much for grace to say, in the name of Jesus, 'The Father abiding in me doeth the work.'

Greater Works

'Verily, verily, I say unto you, He that believeth on Me, the works *that I do* shall *he do also*; and greater works *shall he do*; because I go unto the Father. And whatsoever ye shall ask in My name, *that will I do*, that the Father may be glorified in the Son. If ye shall ask anything in My name, *that will I do*.' – JOHN 14:12–14.

In the words (v. 10), 'The Father abiding in Me doeth the works,' Christ had revealed the secret of His and of all Divine service – man yielding himself for God to dwell and to work in him. When Christ now promises, '"He that believeth on Me, the works that I do shall he do also,' the law of the Divine inworking remains unchanged. In us, as much as in Him, one might even say a thousand times more than with Him, it must still ever be: The Father in me doeth the works. With Christ and with us, it is 'the same God who worketh all in all'.

How this is to be, is taught us in the words, 'he that believeth on Me'. That does not only mean for salvation, as a Saviour from sin. But much more. Christ had just said (vv. 10, 11), '*Believe* Me that *I am in the Father*, and *the Father in Me*: the Father *abiding in Me* doeth the works.' We need to believe in Christ as Him in and through whom the Father unceasingly works. To believe in Christ is to receive Him into the heart. When we see

37

the Father's working inseparably connected with Christ, we know that to believe in Christ, and receive Him into the heart, is to receive the Father dwelling in Him and working through Him. The works His disciples are to do cannot possibly be done in any other way than His own were done.

This becomes still more clear from what our Lord adds: 'And greater works shall he do; because I go unto the Father.' What the greater works are, is evident. The disciples at Pentecost with three thousand baptized, and multitudes added to the Lord; Philip at Samaria, with the whole city filled with joy; the men of Cyprus and Cyrene, and, later on, Barnabas at Antioch, with much people added to the Lord; Paul in his travels, and a countless host of Christ's servants down to our day, have, in the ingathering of souls, done what the Master condescendingly calls greater works than He did in the days of His humiliation and weakness.

The reason why it should be so our Lord makes plain, 'because I go to the Father'. When He entered the glory of the Father, all power in heaven and on earth was given to Him as our Redeemer. In a way more glorious than ever the Father was to work through Him; and He then to work through His disciples. Even as His own work on earth, in the days of the weakness of the flesh, had been in a power received from the Father in heaven, so His people, in their weakness, would do works like His, and greater works in the same way, through a power received from heaven. The law of the Divine working is unchangeable: God's work can only be done by God Himself. It is as we see this in Christ, and receive Him in this capacity, as the One in and through whom God works all, and so yield ourselves wholly to the Father working in Him and in us, that we shall do greater works than He did.

The words that follow bring out still more strongly the great truths we have been learning, that it is our Lord Himself who will work all in us, even as the Father did in Him, and that our posture is to be exactly what His was, one of entire receptivity and dependence. 'Greater works shall *he do*, because I go to the Father, and whatsoever ye shall ask in My name, *that will I do*.' Christ connects the greater works the believer is to do, with the promise that *He will do* whatever the believer asks. Prayer in the name of Jesus will be the expression of that dependence that waits on Him for His working, to which He gives the promise: Whatsoever ye ask, I will do, in you and through you. And when He adds, 'that the Father may be glorified in the Son', He reminds us how He had glorified the Father, by yielding to Him as Father, to work all His work in Himself as Son. In heaven Christ would still glorify the Father, by receiving from the Father the power, and working in His disciples what the Father would. The creature, as the Son Himself, can give the Father no higher glory than yielding to Him to work all. The believer can glorify the Father in no other way than the Son, by an absolute and unceasing dependence on the Son, in whom the Father works, to communicate and work in us all the Father's work. 'If ye shall ask anything in My name, *that will I do*,' and so ye shall do greater works.

Let every believer strive to learn the one blessed lesson. I am to do the works I have seen Christ doing; I may even do greater works as I yield myself to Christ exalted on the throne, in a power He had not on earth; I may count on Him working in me according to that power. My one need is the spirit of dependence and waiting, and prayer and faith, that Christ abiding in me will do the works, even whatsoever I ask.

1. How was Christ able to work the works of God? By God abiding in Him! How can I do the works of Christ? By Christ abiding in me!

2. How can I do greater works than Christ? By believing, not only in Christ, the Incarnate and Crucified, but Christ triumphant on the throne.

3. In work eveything depends, O believer, on the life, the inner life, the Divine life. Pray to realise that work is vain except as it is in 'the power of the Holy Spirit' dwelling in thee.

Created in Christ Jesus for Good Works

'By grace have ye been saved through faith; *not of works*, lest any man should glory. For we are His workmanship, created in Christ Jesus *for good works*, which God afore prepared that we should walk in them.' – EPH. 2:10.

We have been saved, not *of* works, but *for* good works. How vast the difference! How essential the apprehension of that difference to the health of the Christian life. Not *of* works which we have done, as the source whence salvation comes, have we been saved. And yet *for* good works, as the fruit and outcome of salvation, as part of God's work in us, the one thing for which we have been created anew. As worthless as are our works in procuring salvation, so infinite is their worth as that for which God has created and prepared us. Let us seek to hold these two truths in their fulness of spiritual meaning. The deeper our conviction that we have been saved, not of works, but of grace, the stronger the proof we should give that we have indeed been saved for good works.

'Not of works, for ye are God's workmanship.' If works could have saved us, there was no need for our redemption. Because our works were all sinful and vain, God undertook to make us anew – we are now His workmanship, and all the good works we do are His workmanship too. 'His workmanship, created us anew in Christ Jesus.' So complete had been the ruin of sin, that God had to do the work of creation over again in Christ Jesus. In Him, and especially in His resurrection from the dead, He created us anew, after His own image, into the likeness of the life which Christ had lived. In the power of that life and resurrection, we are able, we are perfectly fitted, for doing good works. As the eye, because it was *created* for the light, is most perfectly adapted for its work, as the vine-branch, because it was *created* to bear grapes, does its work so naturally, we who have been *created* in Christ Jesus for good work, may rest assured that a Divine capacity for good works is the very law of our being. If we but know and believe in this our destiny, if we but live our life in Christ Jesus, as we were new created in Him, we can, we will, be fruitful unto every good work.

'Created for good works, which God hath afore prepared that we should walk in them.' We have been prepared for the works, and the works prepared for us. To understand this, think of how God foreordained His servants of old, Moses and Joshua, Samuel and David, Peter and Paul, for the work He had for them, and foreordained equally the works for them. The feeblest member of the body is equally cared for by the Head as the most honoured. The Father has prepared for the humblest of His children their works as much as for those who are counted chief. For every child God has a life-plan, with work apportioned just according to the power, and grace provided just according to the work. And so just as strong and clear as the teaching, *salvation not of works*, is its blessed counterpart, *salvation for good works*, because God created us for them, and even prepared them for us.

And so the Scripture confirms the double lesson this

little book desires to bring you. The one, that good works are God's object in the new life He has given you, and ought therefore to be as distinctly your object. As every human being was created for work, and endowed with the needful powers, and can only live out a true and healthy life by working, so every believer exists to do good works, that in them his life may be perfected, his fellow-men may be blessed, his Father in heaven be glorified. We educate all our children with the thought that they must have their work in the world: when shall the Church learn that its great work is to train every believer to take his share in God's great work, and to abound in the good works for which he was created? Let each of us seek to take in the deep spiritual truth of the message, 'Created in Christ Jesus for good works, which God hath afore prepared' for each one, and which are waiting for him to take up and fulfil.

The other lesson – that waiting on God is the one great thing needed on our part if we would do the good works God has prepared for us. Let us take up into our hearts these words in their Divine meaning: We are God's work-manship. Not by one act in the past, but in a continuous operation. We are created for good works, as the great means for glorifying God. The good works are prepared for each of us, that we might walk in them. Surrender to and dependence upon God's working is our one need. Let us consider how our new creation for good works is all in Christ Jesus, and abiding in Him, believing on Him, and looking for His strength alone will become the habit of our soul. Created for good works! will reveal to us at once the Divine command and the sufficient power to live a life in good works.

Let us pray for the Holy Spirit to work the word into the very depths of our consciousness: Created in Christ Jesus for good works! In its light we shall learn what a glorious destiny, what an infinite obligation, what a perfect capacity is ours.

1. Our creation in Adam was for good works. It resulted in entire failure. Our new creation in Christ is for good works again. But with this difference: perfect provision has been made for securing them.

2. Created by God for good works; created by God in Christ Jesus; the good works prepared by God for us — let us pray for the Holy Spirit to show us and impart to us all this means.

3. Let the life in fellowship with God be true; the power for the work will be sure. As the life, so the work.

Work, for God
works in You

'*Work out* your own salvation with fear and trembling; for *it is God which worketh in you* both to will and to work, for His good pleasure.' – PHIL. 2:12, 13.

In our last chapter we saw what salvation is. It is our being God's workmanship, created in Christ Jesus for good works. It includes, as one of its chief and essential elements, all that treasury of good works which God afore prepared that we should walk in them. In the light of this thought we get the true and full meaning of to-day's text. Work out your own salvation, such as God has meant it to be, a walk in all the good works which God has prepared for you. Study to know exactly what the salvation is God has prepared for you, all that He has meant and made it possible for you to be, and work it out with fear and trembling. Let the greatness of this Divine and most holy life, hidden in Christ, your own absolute importance, and the terrible dangers and temptations besetting you, make you work in fear and trembling.

And yet, that fear need never become unbelief, nor that trembling discouragement, for it is God which worketh in you. Here is the secret of a power that is absolutely sufficient for everything we have to do, of a perfect assurance that we can do all that God really means us to do. God works in us both to will and to work. First, *to will*; He gives the insight into what is to be done, the desire that makes the work pleasure, the firm purpose of the will that masters the whole being, and makes it ready and eager for action. And then *to work*. He does not work to will, and then leave us unaided to work it out ourselves. The will may have seen and accepted the work, and yet the power be lacking to perform. The renewed will of Romans 7, delighted in God's law, and yet the man was impotent *to do*, until in Romans 8:2–4, by the law of the Spirit of life in Christ Jesus, he was set free from the law of sin and death; then first could the righteousness of the law be fulfilled in him, as one who walked not after the flesh but after the Spirit.

One great cause of the failure of believers in their work is that, when they think that God has given them *to will*, they undertake *to work* in the strength of that will. They have never learnt the lesson, that because God has created us in Christ Jesus for good works, and has afore prepared the good works in which we are to walk, He must needs, and will most certainly, Himself work them all in us. They have never listened long to the voice speaking, 'It is God which worketh in you.'

We have here to do with one of the deepest, most spiritual, and most precious truths of Scripture – the unceasing operation of Almighty God in our heart and life. In virtue of the very nature of God, as a Spiritual Being not confined to any place, but everywhere present, there can be no spiritual life but as it is upheld by His personal indwelling.

In the man Christ Jesus the working of the Father in Him was the source of all He did. In the new man, created in Christ Jesus, the unceasing dependence on the Father is our highest privilege, our true nobility. This is indeed fellowship with God: God Himself working in us to will and to do.

Let us seek to learn the true secret of working for God. It is not, as many think, that we do our best, and then leave God to do the rest. By no means. But it is this, that we know that God's working His salvation in us is the secret of our working it out. That salvation includes every work we have to do. The faith of God's working in us is the measure of our fitness to work effectively. The promises, 'According to your faith be it unto you,' and 'All things are possible to him that believeth,' have their full application here. The deeper our faith in God's working in us, the more freely will the power of God work in us, the more true and fruitful will our work be.

Perhaps some Sunday school worker reads this. Let me ask, Have you really believed that your only power to do God's work is as one who has been created in Christ Jesus for good works, as one in whom God Himself works to will and to work? Have you yielded yourself to wait for that working? Do you work because you know God works in you? Say not that these thoughts are too high. The work of leading young souls to Christ is too high for us indeed, but if we live as little children, in believing that God will work all in us, we shall do His work in His strength. Pray much to learn and practise the lesson in all you do: Work, for God worketh in you.

1. I think we begin to feel that the spiritual apprehension of this great truth, 'God worketh in you,' is what all workers greatly need.

2. The Holy Spirit is the mighty power of God, dwelling in believers for life and for work. Beseech God to show it you, that in all our service our first care must be the daily renewing of the Holy Spirit.

3. Obey the command to be filled with the Holy Spirit. Believe in His indwelling. Wait for His teaching. Yield to His leading. Pray for His mighty working. Live in the Spirit.

4. What the mighty power of God works in us we are surely able to do. Only give way to the power working in you.

Faith working by Love

'In Christ Jesus neither circumcision availeth anything, nor uncircumcision; but faith *working* through love. Through love be servants one to another; for the whole law is fulfilled in this: Thou shalt love thy neighbour as thyself.' – GAL. 5:6, 13.

In Christ Jesus no external privilege avails. The Jew might boast of his circumcision, the token of God's covenant. The Gentile might boast of his uncircumcision, with an entrance into the kingdom free from the Jewish law. Neither availed aught in the kingdom of heaven – nothing but a new creature, in which old things are passed away and all things become new. Or, as we have it in our text – as a description of the life of the new creature – nothing but *faith working by love*, that makes us in love serve one another.

What a perfect description of the new life. First you have faith, as the root, planted and rooted in Christ Jesus. Then as its aim you have works, as the fruit. And then between the two, as the tree, growing downwards into the root and bearing the fruit upward, you have love, with the life-sap flowing through it by which the root brings forth the fruit. Of faith we need not speak here. We have seen how believing on Jesus does the greater works; how the faith in the new creation, and in God working in us, is the secret of all work. Nor need we speak here of works – our whole book aims at securing for them the place in every heart and life that they have in God's heart and in His Word.

We have here to study specially the great truth that all work is to be love, that faith cannot do its work but through love, that no works can have any worth but as they come of love, and that love alone is the sufficient strength for all the work we have to do.

The power for work is love. It was love that moved God to all His work in creation and redemption. It was love that enabled Christ as man to work and to suffer as He did. It is love that can inspire us with the power of a self-sacrifice that seeks not its own, but is ready to live and die for others. It is love that gives us the patience that refuses to give up the unthankful or the hardened. It is love that reaches and overcomes the most hopeless. Both in ourselves and those for whom we labour love is the power for work. Let us love as Christ loved us.

The power for love is faith. Faith roots its life in the life of Christ Jesus, which is all love. Faith knows, even when we cannot realise fully, the wonderful gift that has been given into our heart in the Holy Spirit shedding abroad God's love there. A spring in the earth may often be hidden or stopped up. Until it is opened the fountain cannot flow out. Faith knows that there is a fountain of love within that can spring up unto eternal life, that can flow out as rivers of living waters. It assures us that we can love, that we have a Divine power to love within us, as an unalienable endowment of our new nature.

The power to exercise and show love is work. There is no such thing as power in the abstract; it only acts as it is exercised. Power in repose cannot be found or felt. This is specially true of the Christian graces, hidden as they are amid the weakness of our human nature. It is only by doing that you know that you have; a grace must be acted before we can rejoice in its possession. This is the unspeakable blessedness of work, and makes it so essential to a healthy Christian life that it wakens up and strengthens love, and makes us partakers of its joy.

Faith working by love. In Christ Jesus nothing avails but this. Workers for God! believe this. Practise it. Thank God much for the fountain of eternal love opened within you. Pray fervently and frequently that God may strengthen you with might by the power of His Spirit in your inner man, so that, with Christ dwelling in you, you may be rooted and grounded in love. And live, then, your daily life, in your own home, in all your intercourse with men, in all your work, as a life of Divine love. The ways of love are so gentle and heavenly, you may not learn them all at once. But be of good courage, only believe in the power that worketh in you, and yield yourself to the work of love; it will surely gain the victory.

Faith working by love. In Christ Jesus nothing avails but this. You owe everything to God's love. The salvation you have received is all love. God's one desire is *to fill you with His love*. For His own satisfaction, for your own happiness, for the saving of men. Now, I ask you – Will you not accept God's wonderful offer *to be filled with His love?* Oh! come and give up heart and life to the joy and the service of His love. Believe that the fountain of love is within you; it will begin to flow as you make a channel for it by deeds of love. Whatever work for God you try to do, seek to put love into it. Pray for the spirit of love. Give yourself to live a life of love; to think how you can love those around you, by praying for them, by serving them, by labouring for their welfare, temporal and spiritual. Faith working by love in Christ Jesus, this alone availeth much.

1. 'Faith, Hope, Love: the greatest of these is Love.' There is no faith or hope in God. But God is love. The most Godlike thing is love.

2. Love is the nature of God. When it is shed abroad in our hearts by the Holy Spirit love becomes our new nature. Believe this, give yourself over to it, and act it out.

3. Love is God's power to do His work. Love was Christ's power. To work for God pray earnestly to be filled with love to souls!

Bearing Fruit
in every Good Work

'To walk worthily of the Lord unto all pleasing, bearing fruit in *every good work*, and increasing in the knowledge of God; strengthened with all power, according to the might of His glory, unto all patience.' – COL. 1:10.

There is a difference between fruit and work. Fruit is that which comes spontaneously, without thought or will, the natural and necessary outcome of a healthy life. Work, on the contrary, is the product of effort guided by intelligent thought and will. In the Christian life we have the two elements in combination. All true work must be fruit, the growth and product of our inner life, the operation of God's Spirit within us. And yet all fruit must be work, the effect of our deliberate purpose and exertion. In the words, 'bearing fruit in every good work', we have the practical summing up of the truth taught in some previous chapters. Because God works by His life in us, the work we do is fruit. Because, in the faith of His working, we have to will and to work, the fruit we bear is work. In the harmony between the perfect spontaneity that comes from God's life and Spirit animating us, and our co-operation with Him as His intelligent fellow-labourers, lies the secret of all true work.

In the words that precede our text, 'filled with the

knowledge of His will in all wisdom and spiritual under-standing', we have the human side, our need of know-ledge and wisdom; in the words that follow, 'strengthened with all power, according to the might of His glory', we have the Divine side. God teaching and strengthening, man learning to understand and patiently do His will; such is the double life that will be fruitful in every good work.

It has been said of the Christian life that the natural man must first become spiritual, and then again the spiritual man must become natural. As the whole natural life becomes truly spiritual, all our work will partake of the nature of fruit, the outgrowth of the life of God within us. And as the spiritual again becomes perfectly natural to us, a second nature in which we are wholly at home, all the fruit will bear the mark of true work, calling into full exercise every faculty of our being.

'*Bearing fruit unto every good work.*' The words suggest again the great thought, that as an apple tree or a vine is planted solely for its fruit, so the great purpose of our redemption is that God may have us for His work and service. It has been well said: 'The end of man is an Action and not a Thought, though it were of the noblest.' It is in his work that the nobility of man's nature as ruler of the world is proved. It is for good works that we have been new created in Christ Jesus: it is when men see our good works that our Father in Heaven will be glorified, and have the honour which is His due for His workman-ship. In the parable of the vine our Lord insisted on this: 'He that abideth in Me, and I in him, the same beareth *much fruit.*' 'Herein is My Father glorified, that ye bear *much fruit.*' Nothing is more to the honour of a husband-man than to succeed in raising an abundant crop – much fruit is glory to God.

What need that every believer, even the feeblest branch

of the Heavenly Vine, the man who has only one talent, be encouraged and helped, and even trained, to aim at the much fruit. A little strawberry plant may, in its measure, be bearing a more abundant crop than a large apple tree. The call to be fruitful in every good work is for every Christian without exception. The grace that fits for it, of which the prayer, in which our words are found, speaks, is for every one. Every branch fruitful in every good work – this is an essential part of God's Gospel.

'*Bearing fruit in every good work.*' Let us study to get a full impression of the two sides of this Divine truth. God's first creation of life was in the vegetable kingdom. There it was a life without anything of will or self-effort, all growth and fruit was simply His own direct work, the spontaneous outcome of His hidden working. In the creation of the animal kingdom there was an advance. A new element was introduced – thought and will and work. In man these two elements were united in perfect harmony. The absolute dependence of the grass and the lily on the God who clothes them with their beauty were to be the groundwork of our relationship – Nature has nothing but what it receives from God. Our works are to be fruit, the product of a God-given power. But to this was added the true mark of our God-likeness, the power of will and independent action: all fruit is to be our own work. As we grasp this we shall see how the most absolute acknowledgment of our having nothing in ourselves is consistent with the deepest sense of obligation and the strongest will to exert our powers to the very utmost. We shall learn to study the prayer of our text as those who must seek all their wisdom and strength from God alone. And we shall boldly give ourselves, as those who are responsible for the use of that wisdom and strength, to the diligence and the sacrifice and the effort needed for a life bearing fruit in every good work.

1. Much depends, for quality and quantity, on the healthy life of the tree. The life of God, of Christ Jesus, of His Spirit, the Divine life in you, is strong and sure.

2. That life is love. Believe in it. Act it out. Have it replenished day by day out of the fulness there is in Christ.

3. Let all your work be fruit; let all your willing and working be inspired by the life of God. So will you walk worthily of the Lord with all pleasing.

Always abounding
in the Work of the Lord

'Wherefore, my beloved brethren, be ye stedfast, unmoveable, always abounding in *the work of the Lord*,
forasmuch as ye know that your labour is not in vain
in the Lord.' – 1 COR. 15:58.

We all know the fifteenth chapter of 1 Corinthians, in its
Divine revelation of the meaning of Christ's resurrection, with all the blessings of which it is the source.

It gives us a living Saviour, who revealed Himself to
His disciples on earth, and to Paul from heaven. It
secures to us the complete deliverance from all sin. It is
the pledge of His final victory over every enemy, when
He gives up the kingdom to the Father, and God is all
in all. It assures us of the resurrection of the body, and
our entrance on the heavenly life. Paul had closed his
argument with his triumphant appeal to Death and Sin
and the Law: 'O Death, where is thy victory? The sting
of Death is Sin, and the power of Sin is the Law. But
thanks be to God, which giveth us the victory through
our Lord Jesus Christ.' And then follows, after fifty-
seven verses of exultant teaching concerning the mystery
and the glory of the resurrection life in our Lord and His
people, just one verse of practical application: '*Wherefore*, my beloved brethren, be ye stedfast, unmoveable,

always abounding in the work of the Lord.' The faith in a risen, living Christ, and in all that His resurrection is to us in time and eternity, is to fit us for, is to prove itself in – abounding work for our Lord!

It cannot be otherwise. Christ's resurrection was His final victory over sin, and death, and Satan, and His entrance upon His work of giving the Spirit from heaven and extending His kingdom throughout the earth. Those who shared the resurrection joy at once received the commission to make known the joyful news. It was so with Mary and the women. It was so with the disciples the evening of the resurrection day. 'As the Father sent Me, I send you.' It was so with all to whom the charge was given: 'Go into all the world, preach the Gospel to every creature.' The resurrection is the beginning and the pledge of Christ's victory over all the earth. That victory is to be carried out to its complete manifestation through His people. The faith and joy of the resurrection life are the inspiration and the power for the work of doing it. And so the call comes to all believers without exception: 'Wherefore, my beloved brethren, be ye always abounding in the work of the Lord!'

'*In the work of the Lord.*' The connection tells us at once what that work is. Nothing else, nothing less than, telling others of the risen Lord, and proving to them what new life Christ has brought to us. As we indeed know and acknowledge Him as Lord over all we are, and live in the joy of His service, we shall see that the work of the Lord is but one work – *that of winning men to know and bow to Him.* Amid all the forms of lowly, living, patient service, this will be the one aim, in the power of the life of the risen Lord, to make Him Lord of all.

This work of the Lord is no easy one. It cost Christ His life to conquer sin and Satan and gain the risen life. It will cost us our life, too – the sacrifice of the life of nature.

It needs the surrender of all on earth to live in the full power of resurrection newness of life. The power of sin, and the world, in those around us is strong, and Satan does not yield his servants an easy prey to our efforts. It needs a heart in close touch with the risen Lord, truly living the resurrection life, to be stedfast, unmoveable, *always abounding* in the work of the Lord. But that is a life that can be lived – because Jesus lives.

Paul adds: 'Forasmuch as ye know that your labour is not vain in the Lord.' I have spoken more than once of the mighty influence that the certainty of reward for work, in the shape of wages or riches, exerts on the millions of earth's workers. And shall not Christ's workers believe that, with such a Lord, their reward is sure and great? The work is often difficult and slow, and apparently fruitless. We are apt to lose heart, because we are working in our strength and judging by our expectations. Let us listen to the message: 'O ye children of the resurrection life, be ye always abounding in the work of the Lord, forasmuch as ye know your labour is not vain in the Lord.' 'Let not your hands be weak; your work shall be rewarded.' 'You *know* that your labour is not vain in the Lord.'

'*In the Lord.*' The expression is a significant one. Study it in Romans 16, where it occurs ten times, where Paul uses the expressions: 'Receive her in the Lord'; 'my fellow-worker in Christ Jesus'; 'who are in Christ, in the Lord'; 'beloved in the Lord'; 'approved in Christ'; 'who labour in the Lord'; 'chosen in the Lord'. The whole life and fellowship and service of these saints had the one mark – they were, their labours were, in the Lord. Here is the secret of effectual service. Your labour is not 'in vain *in the Lord*'. As a sense of His presence and the power of His life is maintained, as all works are wrought in Him, His strength works in our weakness; our labour

59

cannot be in vain in the Lord. Christ said: 'He that abideth *in Me*, and I in him, the same bringeth forth much fruit.' Oh! let not the children of this world, with their confidence that the masters whose work they are doing will certainly give them their due reward, put the children of light to shame. Let us rejoice and labour in the confident faith of the word: 'Your labour is not in vain in the Lord. Wherefore, beloved brethren, be ye always abounding in the work of the Lord.'

1. Our faith in a risen, living Christ, and in all that His resurrection is to us in time and eternity, is to prove itself in abounding work for the Lord.

2. Rejoice! Your work in the Lord is not in vain. Do not yield to Satan who seeks to discourage and thwart your efforts.

Abounding Grace
for Abounding Work

'And God is able to make all grace abound unto you, that ye may *abound unto every good work*.' – 2 COR. 9:8.

In our previous meditation we had the great motive to abounding work – the spirit of triumphant joy which Christ's resurrection inspires as it covers the past and the future. Our text to-day assures us that for this abounding work we have the ability provided: God is able to make all grace abound, that we may abound to all good works. Every thought of abounding grace is to be connected with the abounding in good works for which it is given. And every thought of abounding work is to be connected with the abounding grace that fits for it.

Abounding grace has *abounding work for its aim*. It is often thought that grace and good works are at variance with each other. This is not so. What Scripture calls the works of the law, our own works, the works of righteousness which we have done, dead works – works by which we seek to merit or to be made fit for God's favour, these are indeed the very opposite of grace. But they are also the very opposite of the good works which spring from grace, and for which alone grace is bestowed. As irreconcilable as are the works of the law with the freedom of grace, so essential and indispensable are the

61

works of faith, good works, to the true Christian life. God makes grace to abound, that good works may abound. The measure of true grace is tested and proved by the measure of good works. God's grace abounds in us that we may abound in good works. We need to have the truth deeply rooted in us: Abounding grace has *abounding work for its aim*.

And abounding work needs *abounding grace as its source and strength*. There often is abounding work without abounding grace. Just as any man may be very diligent in an earthly pursuit, or a heathen in his religious service of an idol, so men may be very diligent in doing religious work in their own strength, with but little thought of that grace which alone can do true, spiritual, effective work. For all work that is to be really acceptable to God, and truly fruitful, not only for some visible result here on earth, but for eternity, the grace of God is indispensable. Paul continually speaks of his own work as owing everything to the grace of God working in him: 'I laboured more abundantly than they all: yet not I, but the grace of God which was with me' (1 Cor. 15:10). 'According to the gift of that grace of God which was given me according to the working of His power' (Eph. 3:7). And he as frequently calls upon Christians to exercise their gifts 'according to the grace that was given us' (Rom. 12:6). 'The grace given according to the measure of the gift of Christ' (Eph. 4:7). It is only by the grace of God working in us that we can do what are truly good works. It is only as we seek and receive abounding grace that we can abound in every good work.

'God is able to make all grace abound unto you, that ye may abound in all good works.' With what thanksgiving every Christian ought to praise God for the abounding grace that is thus provided for him. And with what humiliation to confess that the experience of, and the surrender to, that abounding grace has been so defective. And with what confidence to believe that a life abounding in good works is indeed possible, because the abounding grace for it is so sure and so Divinely sufficient. And then, with what simple childlike dependence to wait upon God day by day to receive the more grace which He gives to the humble.

Child of God! do take time to study and truly apprehend God's purpose with you, *that you abound in every good work!* He means it! He has provided for it! Make the measure of your consecration to Him nothing less than His purpose for you. And claim, then, nothing less than the abounding grace He is able to bestow. Make His omnipotence and His faithfulness your confidence. And live ever in the practice of continual prayer and dependence upon His power working in you. This will make you abound in every good work. According to your faith be it unto you.

Christian worker, learn here the secret of all failure and all success. Work in our own strength, with little prayer and waiting on God for His spirit, is the cause of failure. The cultivation of the spirit of absolute impotence and unceasing dependence will open the heart for the workings of the abounding grace. We shall learn to ascribe all we do to God's grace. We shall learn to measure all we have to do by God's grace. And our life will increasingly be in the joy of God's making His grace to abound in us, and our abounding in every good work.

1. 'That ye may abound to every good work.' Pray over this now till you feel that this is what God has prepared for you.

2. If your ignorance and feebleness appear to make it impossible, present yourself to God, and say you are

willing, if He will enable you, to abound in good works, to be a branch that brings forth much fruit.

3. Take into your heart, as a living seed, the precious truth: God is able to make all grace abound in you. Trust His power and His faithfulness (Rom. 4:20, 21; I Thess. 5:24).

4. Begin at once by doing lowly deeds of love. As the little child in the kindergarten: *Learn by doing*.

In the Work of Ministering

'And He gave some to be apostles; and some, prophets; and some, evangelists; and some, pastors and teachers; for the perfecting of the saints, unto *the work of ministering*, unto the building up of the body of Christ.' – EPH. 4:11, 12.

The object with which Christ when He ascended to heaven bestowed on His servants the various gifts that are mentioned is three-fold. Their first aim is – *for the perfecting of the saints*. Believers as saints are to be led on in the pursuit of holiness until they 'stand perfect and complete in all the will of God'. It was for this Epaphras laboured in prayer. It is of this Paul writes: 'Whom we preach, teaching every man in all wisdom, that we may present every man perfect in Christ' (Col. 4:12, 1:28).

This perfecting of the saints is, however, only a means to a higher end: *unto the work of ministering*, to fit all the saints to take their part in the service to which every believer is called. It is the same word as is used in texts as these: 'They ministered to Him of their substance'; 'Ye ministered to the saints, and do minister' (Luke 4:39, 8:3; 1 Cor. 16:15; Heb. 6:10; 1 Pet. 4:11).

And this, again, is also a means to a still higher end: *unto the building up of the body of Christ*. As every member of our body takes its part in working for the health and growth and maintenance of the whole, so every member of the body of Christ is to consider it his first great duty to take part in all that can help to build up the body of Christ. And this, whether by the helping and strengthening of those who are already members, or the ingathering of those who are to belong to it. And the great work of the Church is, through its pastors and teachers, so to labour for *the perfecting of the saints* in holiness and love and fitness for service, that every one may take his part in *the work of ministering*, that so *the body of Christ may be built up* and perfected.

Of the three great objects with which Christ has given His Church apostles and teachers, the work of ministering stands thus in the middle. On the one hand, it is preceded by that on which it absolutely depends – *the perfecting of the saints*. On the other, it is followed by that which it is meant to accomplish – *the building up of the body of Christ*. Every believer without exception, every member of Christ's body, is called to take part in the work of ministering. Let every reader try and realise the sacredness of his holy calling.

Let us learn what the qualification is for our work. 'The perfecting of the saints' prepares them for the 'work of ministering'. It is the lack of true sainthood, of true holiness, that causes such lack and feebleness of service. As Christ's saints are taught and truly learn what conformity to Christ means, a life like His, given up in self-sacrifice for the service and salvation of men, as His humility and love, His separation from the world and devotion to the fallen, are seen to be the very essence and blessedness of the life He gives, the work of ministering, the ministry of love, will become the one thing we live for. Humility and Love – these are the two great virtues of the saint – they are the two great powers for the work of ministering. Humility makes us willing to serve; love makes us wise to know how to do it. Love is inventive; it seeks patiently, and suffers long, until it finds a way to reach its object. Humility and love are equally turned away from self and its claims. Let us pray, let the Church labour for 'the perfecting of the saints' in humility and love, and the Holy Spirit will teach us how to minister.

Let us look at what the great work is the members of Christ have to do. It is to minister to each other. Place yourself at Christ's disposal for service to your fellow-Christians. Count yourself their servant. Study their interest. Set yourself actively to promote the welfare of the Christians round you. Selfishness may hesitate, the feeling of feebleness may discourage, sloth and ease may raise difficulties – ask your Lord to reveal to you His will, and give yourself up to it. Round about you there are Christians who are cold and worldly and wandering from their Lord. Begin to think what you can do for them. Accept as the will of the Head that you as a member should care for them. Pray for the Spirit of love. Begin somewhere – only begin, and so not continue hearing and thinking while you do nothing. Begin 'the work of ministering' according to the measure of the grace you have. He will give more grace.

Let us believe in the power that worketh in us as sufficient for all we have to do. As I think of the thumb and finger holding the pen with which I write this, I ask, How is it that during all these seventy years of my life they have always known just to do my will? It was because the life of the head passed into and worked itself out in them. 'He that believeth on Me,' as his Head working in him, 'the works that I do shall he do also.' Faith in Christ, whose strength is made perfect in our weakness, will give the power for all we are called to do.

Let us cry to God that all believers may waken up to

the power of this great truth: *Every member of the body is to live wholly for the building up of the body.*

1. To be a true worker the first thing is close, humble fellowship with Christ the Head, to be guided and empowered by Him.

2. The next is humble, loving fellowship with Christ's members, serving one another in love.

3. This prepares and fits for service in the world.

According to the Working of each several Part

'That we may grow up in all things into Him, which is the Head, even Christ; from whom all the body fitly framed and knit together through that which *every joint* supplieth, *according to the working in due measure of each several part*, maketh the increase of the body unto the building up of itself in love.' – EPH. 4:15, 16.

The Apostle is here speaking of the growth, the increase, the building up of the body. This growth and increase has, as we have seen, a double reference. It includes both the spiritual uniting and strengthening of those who are already members, so as to secure the health of the whole body; and also the increase of the body by the addition of all who are as yet outside of it, and are to be gathered in. Of the former we spoke in the previous chapter – the mutual interdependence of all believers, and the calling to care for each other's welfare. In this chapter we look at the growth from the other side – the calling of every member of Christ's body to labour for its increase by the labour of love that seeks to bring in them who are not yet of it. This increase of the body and building up of itself in love can only be by the working in due measure of each several part.

Think of the body of a child; how does it reach the

69

stature of the full-grown man? In no other way but by the working in due measure of every part. As each member takes its part, by the work it does in seeking and taking and assimilating food, the increase is made by its building up itself. Not from without, but from within, comes the work that assures the growth. In no other way can Christ's body attain to the stature of the fulness of Christ. As it is into Christ the Head we grow up, and from Christ the Head that the body maketh increase of itself, so it is all through that which every joint supplieth, according to the working in due measure of each several part. Let us see what this implies.

The body of Christ is to consist of all who believe in Him throughout the world. There is no possible way in which these members of the body can be gathered in, but by the body building itself up in love. Our Lord has made Himself, as Head, absolutely dependent on His members to do this work. What nature teaches us of our own bodies, Scripture teaches us of Christ's body. The head of a child may have thought and plans of growth – they will all be vain, except as the members all do their part in securing that growth. Christ Jesus has committed to His Church the growth and increase of His body. He asks and expects that as wholly as He the Head lives for the growth and welfare of the body, every member of His body, the very feeblest, shall do the same, to the building up of the body in love. Every believer is to count it his one duty and blessedness to live and labour for the increase of the body, the ingathering of all who are to be its members.

What is it that is needed to bring the Church to accept this calling, and to train and help the members of the body to know and fulfil it? One thing. We must see that the new birth and faith, that all insight into truth, with all resolve and surrender and effort to live according to it, is only a preparation for our true work. What is needed is that in every believer Jesus Christ be so formed, so dwell in the heart, that His life in us shall be the impulse and inspiration of our love to the whole body, and our life for it. It is because self occupies the heart that it is so easy and natural and pleasing to care for ourselves. When Jesus Christ lives in us, it will be as easy and natural and pleasing to live wholly for the body of Christ. As readily and naturally as the thumb or fingers respond to the will and movement of the head will the members of Christ's body respond to the Head, as the body grows up into Him, and from Him maketh increase of itself.

1. The Head of the body is entirely dependent on the service of the members.

2. Not only the Lord, but a perishing world is waiting and calling the Church to gather in and build up His body.

3. As we give ourselves to the work of ministering according to the grace we have, so we may confidently wait for the full revelation of Christ in us as the power to do all He asks of us.

Women adorned
with Good Works

'Let women *adorn themselves*; not with braided hair, and gold or pearls or costly raiment; but *through good works*. Let none be enrolled as a widow under three-score years old, *well reported of for good works*; . . . if she hath *diligently followed every good work*.' – 1 Tim. 2:10, 5:9, 10.

In the three Pastoral Epistles, written to two young pastors to instruct them in regard to their duties, 'good works' are more frequently mentioned than in Paul's other Epistles: 1 Tim. 6 times – 2:11, 3:1, 5:10, 5:10, 5:25, 6:18. In 2 Tim. twice – 2:21, 3:17. In Titus 6 times – 1:16, 2:7, 14, 3:1, 8, 14. In writing to the Churches, as in a chapter like Romans 12, he mentions the individual good work by name. In writing to the pastors he had to use this expression as a summary of what, both in their own life and their teaching of others, they had to aim at. A minister was to be prepared to every good work, furnished completely to every good work, an example of good works. And they were to teach Christians – the women to adorn themselves with good works, diligently to follow every good work, to be well reported of for good works; the men to be rich in good works, zealous of good works, ready to every good work, to be careful and to learn to maintain good works. No portion of God's word presses home more definitely the absolute necessity of good works as an essential, vital element in the Christian life.

Our two texts speak of the good works of Christian women. In the first they are taught that their adorning is to be not with braided hair, and gold or pearls or costly raiment, but, as becomes women preferring godliness, with good works. We know what adornment is. A leafless tree in winter has life; when spring comes it puts on its beautiful garments, and rejoices in the adornment of foliage and blossom. The adorning of Christian women is not to be in hair or pearls or raiment, but in good works. Whether it be the good works that have reference to personal duty and conduct, or those works of beneficence that aim at the pleasing and helping of our neighbour, or those that more definitely seek the salvation of souls – the adorning that pleases God, that gives true heavenly beauty, that will truly attract others to come and serve God too, is what Christian women ought to seek after. John saw the holy city descend from heaven, 'made ready as a bride adorned for her husband'. 'The fine linen is the righteous acts of the saints' (Rev. 21:2, 19:8). Oh! that every Christian woman might seek so to adorn herself as to please the Lord that loved her.

In the second passage we read of widows who were placed upon a roll of honour in the early Church, and to whom a certain charge was given over the younger women. No one was to be enrolled who was not 'well reported of for good works'. Some of these are mentioned: if she has been known for the careful bringing up of her children, for her hospitality to strangers, for her washing the saints' feet, for her relieving the afflicted; and then there is added, 'if she hath *diligently followed every good work*'. If in her home and out of it, in caring for her own children, for strangers, for saints, for the afflicted, her life has been devoted to good works, she may indeed be counted fit to be an example and guide to others. The standard is a high one. It shows us the place good works took in the early Church. It shows how woman's blessed ministry of love was counted on and encouraged. It shows how, in the development of the Christian life, nothing so fits for rule and influence as a life given to good works.

Good works are part and parcel of the Christian life, equally indispensable to the health and growth of the individual, and to the welfare and extension of the Church. And yet what multitudes of Christian women there are whose active share in the good work of blessing their fellow-creatures is little more than playing at good works. They are waiting for the preaching of a full gospel, which shall encourage and help and compel them to give their lives so to work for their Lord, that they too may be well reported of as diligently following every good work. The time and money, the thought and heart given to jewels or costly raiment will be redeemed to its true object. Religion will no longer be a selfish desire for personal safety, but the joy of being like Christ, the helper and saviour of the needy. Work for Christ will take its true place as indeed the highest form of existence, the true adornment of the Christian life. And as diligence in the pursuits of earth is honoured as one of the true elements of character and worth, diligently to follow good works in Christ's service will be found to give access to the highest reward and the fullest joy of the Lord.

1. We are beginning to awaken to the wonderful place woman can take in church and school and mission. This truth needs to be brought home to every one of the King's daughters, that the adorning in which they are to

attract the world, to please their Lord, and enter His presence, is – good works.

2. Woman, as the image of 'the weakness of God', 'the meekness and gentleness of Christ', is to teach man the beauty and the power of the long-suffering, self-sacrificing ministry of love.

3. The training for the service of love begins in the home life; is strengthened in the inner chamber; reaches out to the needy around, and finds its full scope in the world for which Christ died.

Rich in Good Works

'Charge them that are rich in the present world, that they do good, that they be *rich in good works*, that they be ready to distribute, willing to communicate, laying up for themselves a good foundation against the time to come, that they may lay hold on the life which is life indeed.' – 1 TIM. 6:18.

If women are to regard good work as their adornment, men are to count them their riches. As good works satisfy woman's eye and taste for beauty, they meet man's craving for possession and power. In the present world riches have a wonderful significance. They are often God's reward on diligence, industry, and enterprise. They represent and embody the life-power that has been spent in procuring them. As such they exercise power in the honour or service they secure from others. Their danger consists in their being of this world, in their drawing off the heart from the living God and the heavenly treasures. They may become a man's deadliest enemy: How hardly shall they that have riches enter the kingdom of heaven!

The Gospel never takes away anything from us without giving us something better in its stead. It meets the desire for riches by the command to be rich in good works. Good works are the coin that is current in God's kingdom: according to these will be the reward in the world to come. By abounding in good works we lay up for ourselves treasures in heaven. Even here on earth they constitute a treasure, in the testimony of a good conscience, in the consciousness of being well-pleasing to God (1 John 3), in the power of blessing others.

There is more. Wealth of gold is not only a symbol of the heavenly riches; it is actually, though so opposite in its nature, a means to it. 'Charge the rich that they do good, that they be ready to distribute, willing to communicate, laying up for themselves a good foundation.' 'Make to yourselves friends by means of the mammon of unrighteousness, that, when it fails, they may receive you into the eternal tabernacles.' Even as the widow's mite, the gifts of the rich, when given in the same spirit, may be an offering with which God is well pleased (Heb. 13:16). The man who is rich in money may become rich in good works, if he follows out the instructions Scripture lays down. The money must not be given to be seen of men, but as unto the Lord. Nor as from an owner, but a steward, who administers the Lord's money, with prayer for His guidance. Nor with any confidence in its power or influence, but in deep dependence on Him who alone can make it a blessing. Nor as a substitute for, or bringing out from that personal work and witness, which each believer is to give. As all Christian work, so our money-giving has its value alone from the spirit in which it is done, even the spirit of Christ Jesus.

What a field there is in the world for accumulating these riches, these heavenly treasures. In relieving the poor, in educating the neglected, in helping the lost, in bringing the Gospel to Christians and heathens in darkness, what investment might be made if Christians sought to be rich in good works, rich toward God. We may well ask the question, What can be done to waken among believers a desire for these true riches? Men have made a science of the wealth of nations, and carefully studied all the laws by which its increase and universal distribution can be promoted. How can the charge to be rich in good works find a response in the hearts that its pursuit shall be as much a pleasure and a passion as the desire for the riches of the present world?

All depends upon the nature, the spirit, there is in man. To the earthly nature, earthly riches have a natural affinity and irresistible attraction. To foster the desire for the acquisition of what constitutes wealth in the heavenly kingdom, we must appeal to the spiritual nature. That spiritual nature needs to be taught and educated and trained into all the business habits that go to make a man rich. There must be the ambition to rise above the level of a bare existence, the deadly contentment with just being saved. There must be some insight into the beauty and worth of good works as the expression of the Divine life – God's working in us and our working for Him; as the means of bringing glory to God; as the source of life and blessing to men; as the laying up of a treasure in heaven for eternity. There must be a faith that these riches are actually within our reach, because the grace and Spirit of God are working in us. And then the outlook for every opportunity of doing the work of God to those around us, in the footsteps of Him who said, 'It is more blessed to give than receive.' Study and apply these principles – they will open the sure road to your becoming a rich man. A man who wants to be rich often begins on a small scale, but never loses an opportunity. Begin at once with some work of love, and ask Christ, who became poor, *that you might be rich*, to help you.

1. What is the cause that the appeal for money for missions meets with such insufficient response? It is

78

because of the low spiritual state of the Church. Christians have no due conception of their calling to live wholly for God and His kingdom.

2. How can the evil be remedied? Only when believers see and accept their Divine calling to make God's kingdom their first care, and with humble confession of their sins yield themselves to God, will they truly seek the heavenly riches to be found in working for God.

3. Let us never cease to plead and labour for a true spiritual awakening throughout the Church.

Prepared unto every Good Work

'If a man therefore cleanse himself from them, he shall be a vessel unto honour, sanctified, meet for the Master's use, *prepared unto every good work*.' – 2 TIM. 2:21.

Paul had spoken of the foundation of God standing sure (2:19), of the Church as the great house built upon that foundation, of vessels, not only of gold, silver, costly and lasting, vessels to honour, but also of wood and of earth, common and perishable, vessels to dishonour. He distinguishes between them of whom he had spoken, who gave themselves to striving about words and to vain babblings, and such as truly sought to depart from all iniquity. In our text he gives us the four steps in the path in which a man can become a vessel unto honour in the great household of God. These are, the cleansing from sin; the being sanctified; the meetness for the Master to use as He will; and last, the spirit of preparedness for every good work. It is not enough that we desire or attempt to do good works. As we need training and care to prepare us for every work we are to do on earth, we need it no less, or rather we need it much more, to be – what constitutes the chief mark of the vessels unto honour – prepared unto every good work.

'*If a man cleanse himself from them*' – from that which characterises the vessels of dishonour – the empty profession leading to ungodliness, against which he had warned. In every dish and cup we use, how we insist upon it that it shall be clean. In God's house the vessels must much more be clean. And every one who would be truly prepared unto every good work must see to this first of all, that he cleanse himself from all that is sin. Christ Himself could not enter upon His saving work in heaven until He had accomplished the cleansing of our sins. How can we become partners in His work, unless there be with us the same cleansing first. Ere Isaiah could say, 'Here am I, send me,' the fire of heaven had touched his lips, and he heard the voice, 'Thy sin is purged.' An intense desire to be cleansed from every sin lies at the root of fitness for true service.

'*He shall be a vessel of honour, sanctified.*' Cleansing is the negative side, the emptying out and removal of all that is impure. *Sanctified*, the positive side, the refilling and being possessed of the Spirit of holiness, through whom the soul becomes God-possessed, and so partakes of His holiness. 'Let us cleanse ourselves from all defilement of flesh and spirit' – this first, then, and so 'perfecting holiness in the fear of the Lord'. In the temple the vessels were not only to be clean, but holy, devoted to God's service alone. He that would truly work for God must follow after holiness: 'a heart established in holiness' (1 Thess. 4:14), a holy habit of mind and disposition, yielded up to God and marked by a sense of His presence, fit for God's work. The cleansing from sin secures the filling with the Spirit.

'*Meet for the Master's use.*' We are vessels for our Lord to use. In every work we do, it is to be Christ using us and working through us. The sense of being a servant, dependent on the Master's guidance, working under the Master's eye, instruments used by Him and His mighty power, lies at the root of effectual service. It maintains

6

that unbroken dependence, that quiet faith, through which the Lord can do His work. It keeps up that blessed consciousness of the work being all His, which leads the worker to become the humbler the more he is used. His one desire is – meet for the Master's use.

'*Prepared unto every good work*.' Prepared. The word not only means equipment, fitness, but also the disposition, the alacrity which keeps a man on the outlook, and makes him earnestly desire and joyfully avail himself of every opportunity of doing his Master's work. As he lives in touch with his Lord Jesus, and holds himself as a cleansed and sanctified vessel, ready for Him to use, and he sees how good works are what he was redeemed for, and what his fellowship with his Lord is to be proved in, they become the one thing he is to live for. He is prepared unto every good work.

1. 'Meet for the Master's use,' that is the central thought. A personal relation to Christ, an entire surrender to His disposal, a dependent waiting to be used by Him, a joyful confidence that He will use us – such is the secret of true work.

2. Let the beginning of your work be a giving of yourself into the hands of the Master, as your living, loving Lord.

Furnished completely unto every Good Work

'Give diligence to present thyself approved unto God, *a workman that needeth not to be ashamed*, handling aright *the word of truth*.' – 2 TIM. 2:15.
'*Every scripture* inspired of God is also profitable for teaching, for reproof, for correction, for instruction which is in righteousness; that the man of God may be complete, *furnished completely unto every good work*.' – 2 TIM. 3:16, 17.

A workman that needeth not to be ashamed is one who is not afraid to have the master come and inspect his work. In hearty devotion to it, in thoroughness and skill, he presents himself approved to him who employs him. God's workers are to give diligence to present themselves approved to Him; to have their work worthy of Him unto all well-pleasing. They are to be as a workman that needeth not to be ashamed. A workman is one who knows his work, who gives himself wholly to it, who is known as a working man, who takes delight in doing his work well. Such every Christian minister, every Christian worker, is to be – a workman that makes a study of it to invite and expect the Master's approval.

'*Handling aright the word of truth*.' The word is a seed, a fire, a hammer, a sword, is bread, is light. Workmen in any of these spheres can be our example. In work for God everything depends upon handling the word aright. Therefore it is that, in the second text quoted above, the personal subjection to the word, and the experience of its power, is spoken of as the one means of our being completely furnished to every good work. God's workers must know that the Scripture is inspired of God, and has the life and life-giving power of God in it. Inspired is Spirit-breathed – as the life in a seed, God's Holy Spirit is in the word. The Spirit in the word and the Spirit in our heart is One. As by the power of the Spirit within us we take the Spirit-filled word we become spiritual men. This word is given *for teaching*, the revelation of the thoughts of God; *for reproof*, the discovery of our sins and mistakes; *for correction*, the removal of what is defective to be replaced by what is right and good; *for instruction which is in righteousness*, the communication of all the knowledge needed to walk before God in His ways. As one yields himself wholly and heartily to all this, and the true Spirit-filled word gets mastery of his whole being, he becomes a man of God, complete and furnished completely to every good work. He becomes a workman approved of God, who needs not to be ashamed, rightly handling the word of God. And so the man of God has the double mark – his own life wholly moulded by the Spirit-breathed word – and his whole work directed by his rightly handling that word.

'*That the man of God may be complete, thoroughly furnished unto every good work.*' In our previous meditation we learnt how in the cleansing and sanctification of the personal life the worker becomes a vessel *meet for the Master's use, prepared unto every good work*. Here we learn the same lesson – it is the man of God who allows God's word to do its work of reproving and correcting and instructing in his own life who will be *complete*, *completely furnished unto every good work.* Complete equipment and readiness for every good work – this is what every worker for God must aim at.

If any worker, conscious of how defective his preparation is, ask how this complete furnishing for every good work is to be attained, the analogy of an earthly workman, who needs not be ashamed, suggests the answer. He would tell us that he owes his success, first of all, to devotion to his work. He gave it his close attention. He left other things to concentrate his efforts on mastering one thing. He made it a life-study to do his work perfectly. They who would do Christ's work as a second thing, not as the first, and who are not willing to sacrifice all for it, will never be complete or completely furnished to every good work.

The second thing he will speak of will be patient training and exercise. Proficiency only comes through painstaking effort. You may feel as if you know not how or what to work aright. Fear not – all learning begins with ignorance and mistakes. Be of good courage. He who has endowed human nature with the wonderful power that has filled the world with such skilled and cunning workmen, will He not much more give His children the grace they need to be His fellow-workers? Let the necessity that is laid upon you – the necessity that you should glorify God, that you should bless the world, that you should through work ennoble and perfect your life and blessedness, urge you to give immediate and continual diligence to be a workman completely furnished unto every good work.

It is only in doing we learn to do aright. Begin working under Christ's training; He will perfect His work in you, and so fit you for your work for Him.

1. The work God is doing, and seeking to have done in the world, is to win it back to Himself.

2. In this work every believer is expected to take part.

3. God wants us to be skilled workmen, who give our whole heart to His work, and delight in it.

4. God does His work by working in us, inspiring and strengthening us to do His work.

5. What God asks is a heart and life devoted to Him in surrender and faith.

6. As God's work is all love, love is the power that works in us, inspiring our efforts and conquering its object.

Zealous of Good Works

'He gave Himself for us, that He might redeem us from all iniquity, and purify us for Himself, a people of His own, *zealous of good works*.' – TIT. 2:14.

In these words we have two truths – what Christ has done to make us His own, and what He expects of us. In the former we have a rich and beautiful summary of Christ's work for us: He gave *Himself for us*, He redeemed us *from all iniquity*, He cleansed *us for Himself*, He took us for a people, *for His own possession*. And all with the one object, that we should be a people *zealous of good works*. The doctrinal half of this wonderful passage has had much attention bestowed on it; let us devote our attention to its practical part – we are to be a people zealous of good works. Christ expects of us that we shall be zealots for good works – ardently, enthusiastically devoted to their performance.

This cannot be said to be the feeling with which most Christians regard good works. What can be done to cultivate this disposition? One of the first things that wakens zeal in work is a great and urgent sense of need. A great need wakens strong desire, stirs the heart and the will, rouses all the energies of our being. It was this sense of need that roused many to be zealous of the law;

they hoped their works would save them. The Gospel has robbed this motive of its power. Has it taken away entirely the need of good works? No, indeed, it has given that urgent need a higher place than before. Christ needs, needs urgently, our good works. We are His servants, the members of His body, without whom He cannot possibly carry on His work on earth. The work is so great – with the hundreds of millions of the unsaved – the work is so great, that not one worker can be spared. There are thousands of Christians to-day who feel that their own business is urgent, and must be attended to, and have no conception of the urgency of Christ's work committed to them. The Church must waken up to teach each believer this.

As urgently as Christ needs our good works the world needs them. There are around you men and women and children who need saving. To see men swept down past us in a river, stirs our every power to try and save them. Christ has placed His people in a perishing world, with the expectation that they will give themselves, heart and soul, to carry on His work of love. Oh! let us sound forth the blessed Gospel message: He gave Himself for us that He might redeem us for Himself, a people of His own, to serve Him and carry on His work – zealous of good works.

A second great element of zeal in work is delight in 'it. An apprentice or a student mostly begins his work under a sense of duty. As he learns to understand and enjoy it, he does it with pleasure, and becomes zealous in its performance. The Church must train Christians to believe that when once we give our hearts to it, and seek for the training that makes us in some degree skilled workmen, there is no greater joy than that of sharing in Christ's work of mercy and beneficence. As physical and mental activity give pleasure, and call for the devotion and zeal of thousands, the spiritual service of Christ can waken our highest enthusiasm.

Then comes the highest motive, the personal one of attachment to Christ our Redeemer: 'The love of Christ constrained us.' The love of Christ to us is the source and measure of our love to Him. Our love to Him becomes the power and the measure of our love to souls. This love, shed abroad in our hearts by the Holy Spirit, this love as a Divine communication, renewed in us by the renewing of the Holy Ghost day by day, becomes a zeal for Christ that shows itself as a zeal for good works. It becomes the link that unites the two parts of our text, the doctrinal and the practical, into one. Christ's love, that gave Himself for us, that redeemed us from all iniquity, that cleansed us for Himself, that made us a people of his own in the bonds of an everlasting loving kindness, that love believed in, known, received into the heart, makes the redeemed soul of necessity zealous in good works.

'*Zealous of good works*!' Let no believer, the youngest, the feeblest, look upon this grace as too high. It is Divine, provided for us and assured in the love of our Lord. Let us accept it as our calling. Let us be sure it is the very nature of the new life within us. Let us, in opposition to all that nature or feeling may say, in faith claim it as an integral part of our redemption – Christ Himself will make it true in us.

1. Christ gave Himself for us. Will you be a zealot of good works for Him?

2. Love senses need, kindles zeal and directs our work.

3. There is no greater joy than in Christ's work.

DAY 22

Ready to every Good Work

'Put them in mind to be *ready to every good work*.' — TIT. 3:1.

'Put them in mind.' The words suggest the need of believers to have the truths of their calling to good works ever again set before them. A healthy tree spontaneously bears its fruit. Even where the life of the believer is in perfect health, Scripture teaches us how its growth and fruitfulness only come through teaching, and the influence that exerts on mind and will and heart. For all who have charge of others the need is great of Divine wisdom and faithfulness to teach and train all Christians, specially young and feeble Christians, to be ready to every good work. Let us consider some of the chief points of such training.

Teach them clearly what good works are. Lay the foundation in the will of God, as revealed in the law, and show them how integrity and righteousness and obedience are the groundwork of Christian character. Teach them how in all the duties and relationships of daily life true religion is to be carried out. Lead them on to the virtues which Jesus specially came to exhibit and teach – humility, meekness and gentleness and love. Open out to them the meaning of a life of love, self-sacrifice, and beneficence – entirely given to think of and care for others. And then carry them on to what is the highest, the true life of good works – the winning of men to know and love God.

Teach them what an essential part of the Christian life good works are. They are not, as many think, a secondary element in the salvation which God gives. They are not merely to be done in token of our gratitude, or as a proof of the sincerity of our faith, or as a preparation for heaven. They are all this, but they are a great deal more. They are the very object for which we have been redeemed: we have been created anew unto good works. They alone are the evidence that man has been restored to his original destiny of working as God works, and with God, and because God works through him. God has no higher glory than His works, and specially His work of saving love. In becoming imitators of God, and walking and working in love, even as Christ loved us and gave Himself for us, we have the very image and likeness of God restored in us. The works of a man not only reveal his life, they develop and exercise, they strengthen and perfect it. Good works are of the very essence of the Divine life in us.

Teach them, too, what a rich reward they bring. All labour has its market value. From the poor man who scarce can earn a shilling a day, to the man who has made his millions, the thought of the reward there is for labour has been one of the great incentives to undertake it. Christ appeals to this feeling when He says, 'Great shall be your reward.' Let Christians understand that there is no service where the reward is so rich as that of God. Work is bracing, work is strength, and cultivates the sense of mastery and conquest. Work wakens enthusiasm, and calls out a man's noblest qualities. In a life of good works the Christian becomes conscious of his Divine ministry of dispensing the life and grace of God to others. They bring us into closer union with God. There is no higher fellowship with God than fellowship in His saving work of love. It brings us into sympathy with Him and His purposes; it fills us with His love; it secures His approval. And great is the reward, too, on those around us. When others are won to Christ, when the weary and the erring and the desponding are helped and made partakers of the grace and life there are in Christ Jesus for them, God's servants share in the very joy in which our blessed Lord found His recompense.

And now the chief thing. *Teach them to believe that it is possible for each of us to abound in good works*. Nothing is so fatal to successful effort as discouragement or despondency. Nothing is a more frequent cause of neglect of good works than the fear that we have not the power to perform them. Put them in mind of the power of the Holy Spirit dwelling in them. Show them that God's promise and provision of strength is always equal to what He demands; that there is always grace sufficient for all the good works to which we are called. Strive to waken in them a faith in 'the power that worketh in us', and in the fulness of that life which can flow out as rivers of living water. Train them to begin at once their service of love. Lead them to see how it is all God working in them, and to offer themselves as empty vessels to be filled with His love and grace. And teach them that as they are faithful in a little, even amid mistakes and short-comings, the acting out of the life will strengthen the life itself, and work for God will become in full truth a second nature.

God grant that the teachers of the Church may be faithful to its commission in regard to all her members – 'Put them in mind to be ready for every good work.' Not only teach them, but train them. Show them the work there is to be done by them; see that they do it; encourage and help them to do it hopefully. There is no part of the office of a pastor more important or more sacred than this, or fraught with richer blessing. Let the aim be nothing less than to lead every believer to live entirely devoted to the work of God in winning men to Him. What a change it would make in the Church and the world!

1. Get a firm hold of the great root-principle. Every believer, every member of Christ's body, has his place in the body solely for the welfare of the whole body.

2. Pastors have been given for the perfecting of the saints with the work of ministering, of serving in love.

3. In ministers and members of the churches, Christ will work mightily if they will wait upon Him.

Careful to maintain
Good Works

'I will that thou affirm these things confidently, to the
end that they which have believed God may be *careful to
maintain good works*. Let our people also *learn to maintain good works* for necessary uses, that they be not un-
fruitful.' – Tɪᴛ. 3:8, 14.

In the former of these passages Paul charges Titus confidently to affirm the truths of the blessed Gospel to the
end, with the express object that all who had believed
should be careful, should make a study of it, *to maintain
good works*. Faith and good works were to be inseparable; the diligence of every believer in good works was
to be a main aim of a pastor's work. In the second
passage he reiterates the instruction, with the expression,
let them learn, suggesting the thought that, as all work on
earth has to be learned, so in the good works of the
Christian life there is an equal need of thought and application and teachableness, to learn how to do them
aright and abundantly.

There may be more than one reader of this little book
who has felt how little he has lived in accordance with
all the teaching of God's word, prepared, thoroughly
furnished, ready unto, zealous of good works. It appears
so difficult to get rid of old habits, to break through the
conventionalities of society, to know how to begin and

really enter upon a life that can be full of good works, to the glory of God. Let me try and give some suggestions that may be helpful. They may aid those who have the training of Christian workers, in showing in what way the teaching and learning of good works may best succeed. Come, young workers all, and listen.

1. *A learner must begin by beginning to work at once.* There is no way of learning an art like swimming or music, a new language, or a trade, but by practice. Let neither the fear that you cannot do it, nor the hope that something will happen that will make it easier for you, keep you back. Learn to do good works, the works of love, by beginning to do them. However insignificant they appear, do them. A kind word, a little help to some one in trouble, an act of loving attention to a stranger or a poor man, the sacrifice of a seat or a place to some one who longs for it – practise these things. All plants we cultivate are small at first. Cherish the consciousness that, for Jesus' sake, you are seeking to do what would please Him. It is only in doing you can learn to do.

2. *The learner must give his heart to the work, must take interest and pleasure in it.* Delight in work ensures success. Let the tens of thousands around you in the world who throw their whole soul into their daily business, teach you how to serve your blessed Master. Think sometimes of the honour and privilege of doing good works, of serving others in love. It is God's own work, to love and save and bless men. He works it in you and through you. It makes you share the spirit and likeness of Christ. It strengthens your Christian character. Without actions, intentions lower and condemn a man instead of raising him. Only as much as you act out, do you really live. Think of the Godlike blessedness of doing good, of communicating life, of making happy. Think of the exquisite joy of growing up into a life of beneficence, and being the

blessing of all you meet. Set your heart upon being a vessel meet for the Master's use, ready to every good work.

3. *Be of good courage, and fear not.* The learner who says I cannot, will surely fail. There is a Divine power working in you. Study and believe what God's word says about it. Let the holy self-reliance of St Paul, grounded on his reliance on Christ, be your example: I can do all things – in Christ which strengtheneth me. Study and take home to yourself the wonderful promises about the power of the Holy Spirit, the abundance of grace, Christ's strength made perfect in weakness, and see how all this can only be made true to you *in working*. Cultivate the noble consciousness that as you have been created to good works by God, He Himself will fit you for them. And believe then that just as natural as it is to any workman to delight and succeed in his profession, it can be to the new nature in you to abound in every good work. Having this confidence, you need never faint.

4. *Above all, cling to your Lord Jesus as your Teacher and Master.* He said: 'Learn of Me, for I am meek and lowly of heart, and ye shall find rest to your souls.' Work as one who is a learner in His school, who is sure that none teaches like Him, and is therefore confident of success. Cling to Him, and let a sense of His presence and His power working in you make you meek and lowly, and yet bold and strong. He who came to do the Father's work on earth, and found it the path to the Father's glory, will teach you what it is to work for God.

To sum up again, for the sake of any who want to learn how to work, or how to work better:

1. Yield yourself to Christ. Lay yourself on the altar, and say you wish to give yourself wholly to live for God's work.

2. Believe quietly that Christ accepts and takes charge of you for His work, and will fit you for it.

3. Pray much that God would open to you the great truth of His own working in you. Nothing else can give true strength.

4. Seek to cultivate a spirit of humble, patient, trustful dependence upon God. Live in loving fellowship with Christ, and obedience to Him. You can count upon His strength being made perfect in your weakness.

As his Fellow-Workers

'We are God's *fellow-workers*: ye are God's building.'
– 1 COR. 3:9.
'And *working together with Him* we intreat also that ye
receive not the grace of God in vain.' – 2 COR. 6:1.

We have listened to Paul's teaching on good works
(Days. 9–22); let us turn now to his personal experience,
and see if we can learn from him some of the secrets of
effective service.

He speaks here of the Church as God's building,
which, as the Great Architect, He is building up into a
holy temple and dwelling for Himself. Of his own work,
Paul speaks as of that of a master builder, to whom a
part of the great building has been given in charge. He
had laid a foundation in Corinth; to all who were working there he said; 'Let each man take heed how he
buildeth thereon.' 'We are God's fellow-workers.' The
word is applicable not only to Paul, but to all God's
servants who take part in His work; and because every
believer has been called to give his life to God's service
and to win others to His knowledge, every, even the
feeblest, Christian needs to have the word brought to
him and taken home: 'We are God's fellow-workers.'
How much it suggests in regard to our working for God!

As to the work we have to do. The eternal God is building for Himself a temple; Christ Jesus, God's Son, is the foundation; believers are the living stones. The Holy Spirit is the mighty power of God through which believers are gathered out of the world, made fit for their place in the temple, and built up into it. As living stones, believers are at the same time the living workmen, whom God uses to carry out His work. They are equally God's workmanship and God's fellow-workers. The work God is doing He does through them. The work they have to do is the very work God is doing. God's own work, in which He delights, on which His heart is set, is saving men and building them into His temple. This is the one work on which the heart of every one who would be a fellow-worker with God must be set. It is only as we know how great, how wonderful, this work of God is – giving life to dead souls, imparting His own life to them, and living in them – that we shall enter somewhat into the glory of our work, receiving the very life of God from Him, and passing it on to men.

As to the strength for the work. Paul says of his work as a mere master builder, that it was 'according to the Grace of God which was given me.' For Divine work nothing but Divine power suffices. The power by which God works must work in us. That power is His Holy Spirit. Study the 2nd chapter of this Epistle, and the 3rd of the Second, and see how absolute was Paul's acknowledgement of his own impotence, and his dependence on the teaching and power of the Holy Spirit. As this great truth begins to live in the hearts of God's workers, that God's work can only be done by God's power in us, we shall feel that our first need every day is to have the presence of God's Spirit renewed within us. The power of the Holy Spirit is the power of love. God is love. All He works for the salvation of men is love; it is love alone that truly conquers and wins the heart. In all God's

99

fellow-workers love is the power that reaches the hearts of men. Christ conquered and conquers still by the love of the cross. Let that mind be in you, O worker, which was in Christ Jesus, the spirit of a love that sacrifices itself to the death, of a humble, patient, gentle love, and you will be made meet to be God's fellow-worker.

As to the relation we are to hold to God. In executing the plans of some great building the master builder has but one care – to carry out to the minutest detail the thoughts of the architect who designed it. He acts in constant consultation with him, and is guided in all by his will; and his instructions to those under him have all reference to the one thing – the embodiment, in visible shape, of what the master mind has conceived. The one great characteristic of fellow-workers with God ought to be that of absolute surrender to His will, unceasing dependence on His teaching, exact obedience to His wishes. God has revealed His plan in His Word. He has told us that His Spirit alone can enable us to enter into His plans, and fully master His purpose with the way He desires to have it carried out. The clearer our insight into the Divine glory of God's work of saving souls, into the utter insufficiency of our natural powers to do the work, into the provision that has been made by which the Divine love can animate us, and the Divine Spirit guide and strengthen us for its due performance, the more we shall feel that a childlike teachableness, a continual looking upward and waiting on God, is ever to be the chief mark of one who is His fellow-labourer. Out of the sense of humility, helplessness, and nothingness there will grow a holy confidence and courage that knows that our weakness need not hinder us, that Christ's strength is made perfect in weakness, that God Himself is working out His purpose through us. And of all the blessings of the Christian life, the most wonderful will be that we are allowed to be – God's fellow-workers!

1. God's fellow-worker! How easy to use the word, and even to apprehend some of the great truths it contains! How little we live in the power and the glory of what it actually involves!

2. Fellow-workers with God! Everything depends upon knowing, in His holiness and love, the God with whom we are associated as partners.

3. He who has chosen us, that in and through us He might do His great work, will fit us for His use.

4. Let our posture be adoring worship, deep dependence, great waiting, full obedience.

According to the Working of His Power

'Whom we preach, warning every man, and teaching every man, that we may present every man perfect in Christ Jesus; whereunto I also labour, striving *according to His working, which worketh in me mightily*.' – COL. 1: 29.

'The mystery of Christ, whereof I was made a minister, according to the gift of that grace of God which was given me *according to the working of His power*.' – EPH. 3:7.

In the words of Paul to the Philippians, which we have already considered (Day 9.), in which he called upon them and encouraged them to work, because it was God who worked in them, we found one of the most pregnant and comprehensive statements of the great truth that it is only by God's working in us that we can do true work. In our texts for today we have Paul's testimony as to his own experience. His whole ministry was to be according to the grace which was given him according to the working of God's power. And of his labour he says that it was a striving according to the power of Him who worked mightily in him.

We find here the same principle we found in our Lord – the Father doing the works in Him. Let every worker who reads this pause, and say – If the ever-blessed Son, if the Apostle Paul, could only do their work according to the working of His power who worked in them mightily, how much more do I need this working of God in me, to fit me for doing His work aright. This is one of the deepest spiritual truths of God's word; let us look to the Holy Spirit within us to give it such a hold of our inmost life, that it may become the deepest inspiration of all our work. I can only do true work as I yield myself to God to work in me.

We know the ground on which this truth rests, 'There is none good but God'; 'There is none holy but the Lord'; 'Power belongeth unto God.' All goodness and holiness and power are only to be found in God, and where He gives them. And He can only give them in the creature, not as something He parts with, but by His own actual presence and dwelling and working. And so God can only work in His people in as far as He is allowed to have complete possession of the heart and life. As our will and life and love are yielded up in dependence and faith, and God is waited on to keep possession and to abide, even as Christ waited on Him, God can work in us.

This is true of all our spiritual life, but specially of our work for God. The work of saving souls is God's own work: none but He can do it. The gift of His Son is the proof of how great and precious He counts the work, and how His heart is set upon it. His love never for one moment ceases working for the salvation of men. And when He calls His children to be partners in His work, He shares with them the joy and the glory of the work of saving and blessing men. He promises to work His work through them, inspiring and energising them by His power working in them. To him who can say with Paul: 'I labour, striving according to His power who worketh in me mightily,' his whole relation to God becomes the counterpart and the continuation of Christ's, a blessed, unceasing, momentary, and most absolute dependence on the Father for every word He spoke and every work He did.

Christ is our pattern. Christ's life is our law and works in us. Christ lived in Paul his life of dependence on God. Why should any of us hesitate to believe that the grace given to Paul of labouring and striving 'according to the working of the power' will be given to us too. Let every worker learn to say – As the power that worked in Christ worked in Paul too, that power works no less in me. There is no possible way of working God's work aright, but by God working it in us.

How I wish that I could take every worker who reads this by the hand, and say – Come, my brother! let us quiet our minds, and hush every thought in God's presence, as I whisper in your ears the wonderful secret: *God is working in you. All the work you have to do for Him, God will work in you.* Take time and think it over. It is a deep, spiritual truth which the mind cannot grasp nor the heart realise. Accept it as a Divine truth from heaven; believe that this word is a seed out of which can grow the very spiritual blessing of which it speaks. And in the faith of the Holy Spirit's making it live within you, say ever again: *God worketh in me.* All the work I have to work for Him, God will work in me.

The faith of this truth, and the desire to have it made true in you, will constrain you to live very humbly and closely with God. You will see how work for God must be the most spiritual thing in a spiritual life. And you will ever anew bow in holy stillness: God is working; God will work in me; I will work for Him according to the power which worketh in me mightily.

1. The gift of the grace of God (Eph. 2:7, 3:7), the power

that worketh in us (Eph. 3:20), the strengthening with might by the Spirit (Eph. 3:16), – the three expressions all contain the same thought of God's working all in us.

2. The Holy Spirit is the power of God. Seek to be filled with the Spirit, to have your whole life led by Him, and you will become fit for God's working mightily in you.

3. 'Ye shall receive the power of the Holy Spirit coming on you.' Through the Spirit dwelling in us God can work in us mightily.

4. What holy fear, what humble watchfulness and dependence, what entire surrender and obedience become us if we believe in God's working in us.

Labouring more Abundantly

'By the grace of God I am what I am: and His grace which was bestowed on me was not in vain; but I *laboured more abundantly* than they all: yet not I but the grace of God which was with me.' – 1 COR. 15:10.

'And He hath said unto me, My grace is sufficient for thee: for my power is made perfect in weakness. . . . In nothing was I behind the chiefest of the apostles, though I am nothing.' – 2 COR. 12:9, 11.

In both of these passages Paul speaks of how he had abounded in the work of the Lord. 'In nothing was I behind the chiefest of the Apostles.' 'I laboured more abundantly than they all.' In both he tells how entirely it was all of God, who worked in Him, and not of himself. In the first he says: 'Not I, but the grace of God which was with me.' And then in the second, showing how this grace is Christ's strength working in us, while we are nothing, he tells us: 'He said unto me: My grace is sufficient for thee: My power is made perfect in weakness.' May God give us 'the Spirit of revelation, enlightened eyes of the heart', to see this wonderful vision, a man who knows himself to be nothing, glorying in his weakness, that the power of Christ may rest on him, and work through him, and who so labours more abundantly than all. What does this teach us as workers for God.

God's work can only be done in God's strength. It is only by God's power, that is, by God Himself working in us, that we can do effective work. Throughout this little book this truth has been frequently repeated. It is easy to accept of it; it is far from easy to see its full meaning, to give it the mastery over our whole being, to live it out. This will need stillness of soul, and meditation, strong faith and fervent prayer. As it is God alone who can work in us, it is equally God *who alone can reveal Himself as the God who works in us.* Wait on Him, and the truth that ever appears to be beyond thy reach will be opened up to thee, through the knowledge of who and what God is. When God reveals Himself as '*God who worketh all in all,*' thou wilt learn to believe and work 'according to the power of Him who worketh in thee mightily.'

God's strength can only work in weakness. It is only when we truly say, *Not I!* that we can fully say, *but the grace of God with me.* The man who said, *In nothing behind the chiefest of the Apostles!* had first learnt to say, *though I am nothing.* He could say: 'I take pleasure in weaknesses, for when I am weak then am I strong.' This is the true relation between the Creator and the creature, between the Divine Father and His child, between God and His servant. Christian worker! learn the lesson of thine own weakness, as the indispensable condition of God's power working in thee. Do believe that to take time and in God's presence to realise thy weakness and nothingness is the sure way to be clothed with God's strength. Accept every experience by which God teaches thee thy weakness as His grace preparing thee to receive His strength. Take pleasure in weaknesses!

God's strength comes in our fellowship with Christ and His service. Paul says: 'I will glory in my weakness, that *the strength of Christ* may rest upon me.' 'I take pleasure

107

in weaknesses *for Christ's sake.*' And he tells how it was when he had besought *the Lord* that the messenger of Satan might depart from him, that He answered: 'My grace is sufficient for thee.' 'Christ is the wisdom and the power of God.' We do not receive the wisdom to know, or the power to do, God's will as something that we can possess and use at discretion. It is in the personal attachment to Christ, in a life of continual communication with Him, that His power rests on us. It is in taking pleasure in weaknesses for Christ's sake that Christ's strength is known.

God's strength is given to faith, and the work that is done in faith. It needs a living faith to take pleasure in weaknesses, and in weakness to do our work, knowing that God is working in us. Without seeing or feeling anything, to go on in the confidence of a hidden power working in us – this is the highest exercise of a life of faith. To do God's own work in saving souls, in persevering prayer and labour; amid outwardly unfavourable circumstances and appearances still to labour more abundantly – this faith alone can do. Let us be strong in faith, giving glory to God. God will show Himself strong towards him whose heart is perfect with Him.

My brother! be willing to yield yourself to the very utmost to God, that His power may rest upon you, may work in you. *Do let God work through you.* Offer yourself to Him for His work as the one object of your life. Count upon His working all in you, to fit you for His service, to strengthen and bless you in it. Let the faith and love of your Lord Jesus, whose strength is going to be made perfect in your weakness, lead you to live even as He did, to do the Father's will and finish His work.

1. Let every minister seek the full personal experience of Christ's strength made perfect in His weakness: this

alone will fit him to teach believers the secret of their strength.

2. Our Lord says: 'My grace, My strength.' It is as, in close personal fellowship and love, we abide in Christ, and have Christ abiding in us, that His grace and strength can work.

3. It is a heart wholly given up to God, to His will and love, that will know His power working in our weakness.

A Doer that worketh
shall be blessed in Doing

'Be ye *doers* of the word, and not hearers only, deluding your own selves. He that looketh into the perfect law, the law of liberty, and so continueth, being not a hearer that forgetteth, but *a doer that worketh*, this man shall be *blessed in doing*.' – JAS. 1:22, 25.

'God created us not to contemplate but to act. He created us in His own image, and in Him there is no Thought without simultaneous Action.' True action is born of contemplation. True contemplation, as a means to an end, always begets action. If sin had not entered there had never been a separation between knowing and doing. In nothing is the power of sin more clearly seen than this, that even in the believer there is such a gap between intellect and conduct. It is possible to delight in hearing, to be diligent in increasing our knowledge of God's word, to admire and approve the truth, even to be willing to do it, and yet to fail entirely in the actual performance. Hence the warning of James, not to delude ourselves with being hearers and not doers. Hence his pronouncing the doer who worketh blessed in his doing.

Blessed in doing. The words are a summary of the teaching of our Lord Jesus at the close of the Sermon on the Mount: '*He that doeth* the will of My Father shall enter the kingdom of heaven.' 'Every one that heareth My words, *and doeth them*, shall be likened unto a wise man.' To the woman who spoke of the blessedness of her who was his mother: 'Yea rather, blessed are they that hear the word of God *and keep it.*' To the disciples in the last night: 'If ye know these things, happy are ye if ye *do them.*' It is one of the greatest dangers in religion that we rest content with the pleasure and approval which a beautiful representation of a truth calls forth, without the immediate performance of what it demands. It is only when conviction has been translated into conduct that we have proof that the truth is mastering us.

A doer that worketh shall be blessed in doing. The doer is blessed. The doing is the victory that overcomes every obstacle; it brings out and confirms the very image of God, the Great Worker; it removes every barrier to the enjoyment of all the blessing God has prepared. We are ever inclined to seek our blessedness in what God gives, in privilege and enjoyment. Christ placed it in what we do, because it is only in doing that we really prove and know and possess the life God has bestowed. When one said, 'Blessed is he that shall eat bread in the kingdom of God,' our Lord answered with the parable of the supper, 'Blessed is he that forsakes all to come to the supper.' The doer is blessed. As surely as it is only in doing that the painter or musician, the man of science or commerce, the discoverer or the conqueror find their blessedness, so, and much more, is it only in keeping the commandments and in doing the will of God that the believer enters fully into the truth and blessedness of deliverance from sin and fellowship with God. Doing is the very essence of blessedness, the highest manifestation, and therefore the fullest enjoyment of the life of God.

A doer that worketh shall be blessed in doing. This was the blessedness of Abraham, of whom we read: 'Thou seest that faith wrought with his works, and by works was faith made perfect.' He had no works without faith; there was faith working with them and in them all. And he had no faith without works: through them his faith was exercised and strengthened and perfected. As his faith, so his blessedness was perfected in doing. It is in *doing* that the doer that worketh is blessed. The true insight into this, as a Divine revelation of the true nature of good works, in perfect harmony with all our experience in the world, will make us take every command, and every truth, and every opportunity to abound in good works as an integral part of the blessedness of the salvation Christ has brought us. Joy and work, work and joy, will become synonymous: we shall no longer be hearers but doers.

Let us put this truth into immediate practice. Let us live for others, to love and to serve them. Let not the fact of our being unused to labours of love, or the sense of ignorance and unfitness, keep us back. Only begin. If you think you are not able to labour for souls, begin with the bodies. Only begin, and go on, and abound. Believe the word, It is more blessed to give than to receive. Pray for and depend on the promised grace. Give yourself to a ministry of love; in the very nature of things, in the example of Christ, in the promise of God you have the assurance: If you know these things, *happy are ye if ye do them*. Blessed is the doer!

1. It is only when conviction has been translated into conduct that we have proof that the truth is mastering us.

2. Blessings flow from doing not hearing.

The Work of Soul-Saving

'My brethren, if any of you do err from the truth, and one convert him, let him know that *he which converteth a sinner* from the error of his ways shall *save a soul* from death, and shall cover a multitude of sins.' – JAS. 5:19.

We sometimes hesitate to speak of men being converted and saved by men. Scripture here twice uses the expression of one man converting another, and once of his saving him. Let us not hesitate to accept it as part of our work, of our high prerogative as the sons of God, to convert and to save men. 'For it is God who worketh in us.'

'*Shall save a soul from death.*' Every workman studies the material in which he works: the carpenter the wood, the goldsmith the gold. 'Our works are wrought in God.' In our good works we deal with souls. Even when we can at first do no more than reach and help their bodies, our aim is the soul. For these Christ came to die. For these God has appointed us to watch and labour. Let us study these. What care a huntsman or a fisherman takes to know the habits of the spoil he seeks. Let us remember that it needs Divine wisdom and training and skill to become winners of souls. The only way to get that training and skill is to begin to work: Christ Himself will teach each one who waits on Him.

In that training the Church with its ministers has a part

to take. The daily experience of ordinary life and teaching prove how often there exist in a man unsuspected powers, which must be called out by training before they are known to be there. When a man thus becomes conscious and master of the power there is in himself he is, as it were, a new creature; the power and enjoyment of life is doubled. Every believer has hidden within himself the power of saving souls. The kingdom of heaven is within us as a seed, and every one of the gifts and graces of the spirit are each also a hidden seed. The highest aim of the ministry is to waken the consciousness of this hidden seed of power to save souls. A depressing sense of ignorance or impotence keeps many back. James writes: 'Let him who converts another *know* that he has saved a soul from death.' Every believer needs to be taught to know and use the wondrous blessed power with which he has been endowed. When God said to Abraham: 'I will bless thee, then shall all the nations of the earth be blessed,' He called him to a faith not only in the blessing that would come to him from above, but in the power of blessing he would be in the world. It is a wonderful moment in the life of a child of God when he sees that the second blessing is as sure as the first.

'*He shall save a soul.*' Our Lord bears the name of Jesus, Saviour. He is the embodiment of God's saving love. Saving souls is His own great work, is His work alone. As our faith in Him grows to know and receive all there is in Him, as He lives in us, and dwells in our heart and disposition, saving souls will become the great work to which our life will be given. We shall be the willing and intelligent instrument through whom He will do His mighty work.

'*If any err, and one convert him, he which converteth a sinner shall save a soul.*' The words suggest personal work. We chiefly think of large gatherings to whom the Gospel

114

is preached; the thought here is of one who has erred and is sought after. We increasingly do our work through associations and organisations. 'If *one* convert him, *he* saveth a soul;' it is the love and labour of some individual believer that has won the erring one back. It is this we need in the Church of Christ – every believer who truly follows Jesus Christ looking out for those who are erring from the way, loving them, and labouring to help them back. Not one of us may say, 'Am I my brother's keeper?' We are in the world only and solely that as the members of Christ's body we may continue and carry out His saving work. As saving souls was and is His work, His joy, His glory, let it be ours, let it be mine too. Let me give myself personally to watch over individuals, and seek to save them one by one.

'*Know that he which converteth a sinner shall save a soul.*' 'If ye *know* these things, happy are ye if you *do* them.' Let me translate these Scripture truths into action; let me give these thoughts shape and substance in daily life; let me prove their power over me, and my faith in them, by *work*. Is there not more than one Christian around me wandering from the way, needing loving help and not unwilling to receive it? Are there not some whom I could take by the hand, and encourage to begin again? Are there not many who have never been in the right way, for some of whom Christ Jesus would use me, if I were truly at His disposal.

If I feel afraid – oh! let me believe that the love of God as a seed dwells within me, not only calling but enabling me actually to do the work. Let me yield myself to the Holy Spirit to fill my heart with that love, and fit me for its service. Jesus the Saviour lives to save; He dwells in me; He will do His saving work through me. '*Know that he which converteth a sinner shall save a soul from death, and cover a multitude of sins.*'

1. More love to souls, born out of fervent love to the Lord Jesus – is not this our great need?

2. Let us pray for love, and begin to love, in the faith that as we exercise the little we have more will be given.

3. Lord! open our eyes to see Thee doing Thy great work of saving men, and waiting to give Thy love and strength into the heart of every willing one. Make each of Thy redeemed a soul-winner.

Praying and Working

'If any man see his brother sinning a sin not unto death, he shall ask, and God will give him life for them that sin not unto death.' – 1 JOHN 5:16.

'Let us consider one another to provoke unto love and good works' – these words in Hebrews express what lies at the very root of a life of good works – the thoughtful loving care we have for each other, that not one may fall away. As it is in Galatians: 'Even if a man be overtaken in a trespass, ye which are spiritual, restore such a one in the spirit of meekness.' Or as Jude writes, apparently of Christians who were in danger of falling away, 'Some save, snatching them out of the fire; and on some have mercy with fear.' As Christ's doing good to men's bodies ever aimed at winning their souls, all our ministry of love must be subordinated to that which is God's great purpose and longing – the salvation unto life eternal.

In this labour of love praying and working must ever go together. At times prayer may reach those whom the words cannot reach. At times prayer may chiefly be needed for ourselves, to obtain the wisdom and courage for the words. At times it may be specially called forth for the soul by the very lack of fruit from our words. As a rule, praying and working must be inseparable – the praying to obtain from God what we need for the soul;

117

the working to bring to it what God has given us. The words of John here are most suggestive as to the power of prayer in our labour of love. It leads us to think of prayer as a personal work; with a very definite object; and a certainty of answer.

Let prayer be a personal effort. *If any man see* his brother *he shall ask*. We are so accustomed to act through societies and associations that we are in danger of losing sight of the duty resting upon each of us to watch over those around him. Every member of my body is ready to serve any other member. Every believer is to care for the fellow-believers who are within his reach, in his church, his house, or social circle. The sin of each is a loss and a hurt to the body of Christ. Let your eyes be open to the sins of your brethren around you; not to speak evil or judge or helplessly complain, but to love and help and care and pray. Ask God to see your brother's sin, in its sinfulness, its danger to himself, its grief to Christ, its loss to the body; but also as within reach of God's compassion and deliverance. Shutting our eyes to the sin of our brethren around us is not true love. See it, and take it to God, and make it part of your work for God to pray for your brother and seek new life for him.

Let prayer be definite. If any man see *his brother sinning* let him ask. We need prayer from a person for a person. Scripture and God's Spirit teach us to pray for all society, for the Church with which we are associated, for nations, and for special spheres of work. Most needful and blessed. But somehow more is needed – to take of those with whom we come into contact, one by one, and make them the subjects of our intercession. The larger supplications must have their place, but it is difficult with regard to them to know when our prayers are answered. But there is nothing that will bring God so near, will test and strengthen our faith, and make us know we are fellow-workers with God, as when we receive an answer to our prayers for individuals. It will quicken in us the new and blessed consciousness that we indeed have power with God. Let every worker seek to exercise this grace of taking up and praying for individual souls.

Count upon an answer. He shall ask, *and God will give him* (the one who prays) *life for them that sin*. The words follow on those in which John had spoken about the confidence we have of being heard, if we ask anything *according to His will*. There is often complaint made of not knowing God's will. But here there is no difficulty. 'He *willeth* that all men should be saved.' If we rest our faith on this will of God, we shall grow strong and grasp the promise. 'He shall ask, and *God will give him life* for them that sin.' The Holy Spirit will lead us, if we yield ourselves to be led by Him, to the souls God would have us take as our special care, and for which the grace of faith and persevering prayer will be given us. Let the wonderful promise: *God will give to him who asks life* for them who sin, stir us and encourage us to our priestly ministry of personal and definite intercession, as one of the most blessed among the good works in which we can serve God and man.

Praying and working are inseparable. Let all who work learn to pray well. Let all who pray learn to work well.

1. To pray Thee confidently, and, if need be, perseveringly, for an individual, needs a close walk with God, and the faith that we can prevail with Him.

2. In all our work for God, prayer must take a much larger place. If God is to work all; if our posture is to be that of entire dependence, waiting for Him to work in us; if it takes time to persevere and to receive in ourselves

what God gives us for others; there needs to be a work and a labouring in prayer.

3. Oh that God would open our eyes to the glory of this work of saving souls, as the one thing God lives for, as the one thing He wants to work in us.

4. Let us pray for the love and power of God to come on us, for the blessed work of soul-winning.

I Know thy Works

'To the angel of the church in Ephesus – in Thyatira – in Sardis – in Philadelphia – in Laodicea write: *I know thy works.*' – REV. 2, 3.

'I know thy works.' These are the words of Him who walketh in the midst of the seven golden candlesticks, and whose eyes are like a flame of fire. As He looks upon the churches, the first thing He sees and judges of is – the works. The works are the revelation of the life and character. If we are willing to bring our works into His holy presence, His words can teach us what our work ought to be.

To Ephesus He says: '*I know thy works*, and thy toil and patience, and that thou canst not bear evil men, and thou hast patience and didst bear for My name's sake, and hast not grown weary. But I have this against thee, that thou hast *left thy first love*. Repent, and *do the first works.*' There was here much to praise – toil, and patience, and zeal that had never grown weary. But there was one thing lacking – the tenderness of the first love.

In His work for us Christ gave us before and above everything His love, the personal tender affection of His heart. In our work for Him He asks us nothing less. There is such a danger of work being carried on, and our even bearing much for Christ's sake, while the freshness of our love has passed away. And that is what Christ seeks. And that is what gives power. And that is what nothing can compensate for. Christ looks for the warm loving heart, the personal affection which ever keeps Him the centre of our love and joy.

Christian workers, see that all your work be the work of love, of tender personal devotion to Christ Jesus.

To Thyatira: '*I know thy works*, and thy love and faith and ministry and patience, and that *the last works are more than the first*. But I have this against thee, that thou sufferest the woman Jezebel, and she teacheth and seduceth My servants.' Here again the works are enumerated and praised: the last had even been more than the first. But then there is one failure: a false toleration of what led to impurity and idolatry. And then He adds of His judgments: 'the churches shall know that I am He which searches the reins and hearts; and *I will give to each one of you according to your works*.'

Along with much of good works there may be some one form of error or evil tolerated which endangers the whole church. In Ephesus there was zeal for orthodoxy, but a lack of love; here love and faith, but a lack of faithfulness against error. If good works are to please our Lord, if our whole life must be in harmony with them, in entire separation from the world and its allurements, we must seek to be what He promised to make us, stablished in every good word and work. Our work will decide our estimate in His judgment.

To Sardis: '*I know thy works*, that thou hast a name to live, and thou art dead. Be watchful and stablish the things that are ready to die: for I have found *no works of thine fulfilled before My God*.'

There may be all the forms of godliness without the power; all the activities of religious organisation without the life. There may be many works, and yet He may say:

I have found no work of thine fulfilled before My God, none that can stand the test and be really acceptable to God as a spiritual sacrifice. In Ephesus it was works lacking in love, in Thyatira works lacking in purity, in Sardis works lacking in life.

To Philadelphia: '*I know thy works*, that thou hast a little power, and *didst keep My word* and didst not deny My name. Because *thou didst keep My word*, I also will keep thee.'

On earth Jesus had said: 'He that *hath My commandments and keepeth them*, he it is that loveth Me. If a man love Me, *he will keep My word*, and My Father will love him.' Philadelphia, the church for which there is no reproof, had this mark: its chief work, and the law of all its work, was, *it kept Christ's word*, not in an orthodox creed only, but in practical obedience. Let nothing less, let this truly, be the mark and spirit of all our work: a keeping of the word of Christ. Full, loving conformity to His will will be rewarded.

To Laodicea: '*I know thy works*, that thou art neither cold nor hot. Thou sayest, I am rich and have gotten riches, and have need of nothing.' There is not a church without its works, its religious activities. And yet the two great marks of Laodicean religion, lukewarmness, and its natural accompaniment, self-complacence, may rob them of their worth. It not only, like Ephesus, teaches us the need of a fresh and fervent love, but also the need of that poverty of spirit, that conscious weakness out of which the absolute dependence on Christ's strength for all our work will grow, and which will no longer leave Christ standing at the door, but enthrone Him in the heart.

'I know thy works.' He who tested the works of the seven churches still lives and watches over us. He is ready in His love to discover what is lacking, to give

123

timely warning and help, and to teach us the path in which our works can be fulfilled before His God. Workers! Let us live and work in Christ's presence. He will teach and correct and help us, and one day give the full reward of all our works because they were His own works in us.

Let us learn the lesson of:

1. Fervent love to Christ.

2. Purity and separation from all evil.

3. The need of true life to give worth to work.

4. Keeping His Word.

5. The poverty of spirit which possesses the kingdom and gives Christ the throne of all.

That God may be Glorified

'If any man *serveth*, let him *serve* as of the strength which God supplieth: that in all things God may be gloried through Jesus Christ, whose is the glory and dominion for ever and ever. Amen.' – 1 PET. 4:11.

Work is not done for its own sake. Its value consists in the object it attains. The purpose of him who commands or performs the work gives it its real worth. And the clearer a man's insight into the purpose, the better fitted will he be to take charge of the higher parts of the work. In the erection of some splendid building, the purpose of the day-labourer may simply be as a hireling to earn his wages. The trained stone-cutter has a higher object: he thinks of the beauty and perfection of the work he does. The master mason has a wider range of thought: his aim is that all the masonry shall be true and good. The contractor for the whole building has a higher aim – that the whole building shall perfectly correspond to the plan he has to carry out. The architect has had a still higher purpose – that the great principles of art and beauty might find their full expression in material shape. With the owner we find the final end – the use to which the grand structure is to be put when he, say, presents the building as a gift for the benefit of his townsmen. All who have worked upon the building honestly have done so

125

with some true purpose. The deeper the insight and the keener the interest in the ultimate design, the more important the share in the work, and the greater the joy in carrying it out.

Peter tells us what our aim ought to be in all Christian service – 'that in all things God may be glorified through Jesus Christ'. In the work of God, a work not to be done for wages but for love, the humblest labourer is admitted to a share in God's plans, and to an insight into the great purpose which God is working out. That purpose is nothing less than this: that God may be glorified. This is the one purpose of God, the great worker in heaven, the source and master of all work, that the glory of His love and power and blessing may be shown. This is the one purpose of Christ, the great worker on earth in human nature, the example and leader of all our work. This is the great purpose of the Holy Spirit, the power that worketh in us, or, as Peter says here, 'the strength that God supplieth'. As this becomes our deliberate, intelligent purpose, our work will rise to its true level, and lift us into living fellowship with God.

'That in all things God may be glorified.' What does this mean? The glory of God is this, that He alone is the Living One, who has life in Himself. Yet not for Himself alone, but, because His life is love, for the creatures as much as for Himself. This is the glory of God, that He is the alone and ever-flowing fountain of all life and goodness and happiness, and that His creatures can have all this only as He gives it and works it in them. His working all in all, this is His glory. And the only glory His creature, His child, can give Him is this – receiving all He is willing to give, yielding to Him to let Him work, and then acknowledging that He has done it. Thus God Himself shows forth His glory in us; in our willing surrender to Him, and our joyful acknowledgment that He does

126

all, we glorify Him. And so our life and work is glorified, as it has one purpose with all God's own work, 'that in all things God may be glorified, whose is the glory for ever and ever'.

See here now the spirit that ennobles and consecrates Christian service according to Peter: 'He that serveth (in ministering to the saints or the needy), let him service *as of the strength which God supplieth.*' Let me cultivate a deep conviction that God's work, down into the details of daily life, can only be done in God's strength, 'by the power of the Spirit working in us'. Let me believe firmly and unceasingly that the Holy Spirit does dwell in me, as the power from on high for all work to be done for on high. Let me in my Christian work fear nothing so much as working in my own human will and strength, and so losing the one thing needful in my work, God working in me. Let me rejoice in the weakness that renders me so absolutely dependent upon such a God, and wait in prayer for His power to take full possession.

'Let him serve as of the strength which God supplieth, *that in all things God may be glorified through Jesus Christ.*' The more you depend on God alone for your strength, the more will He be glorified. The more you seek to make God's purpose your purpose, the more will you be led to give way to His working and His strength and love. Oh! that every, the feeblest, worker might see what a nobility it gives to work, what a new glory to life, what a new urgency and joy in labouring for souls, when the one purpose has mastered us: that in all things God may be glorified through Jesus Christ.

1. The glory of God as Creator was seen in His making man in His own image. The glory of God as Redeemer is seen in the work He carries on for saving men, and bring-ing them to Himself.

2. This glory is the glory of His holy love, casting sin out of the heart, and dwelling there.

3. The only glory we can bring to God is to yield ourselves to His redeeming love to take possession of us, to fill us with love to others, and so through us to show forth His glory.

4. Let this be the one end of our lives – to glorify God; in living to work for Him, 'as of the strength which God supplieth'; and winning souls to know and live for His glory.

5. Lord! teach us to serve in the strength which God supplieth, that God in all things may be glorified through Jesus Christ, whose is the glory for ever and ever. Amen.